The
ELEMENTS
of
HUMOR

SCOTT
DIKKERS

Founder of TheOnion.com

The Tools of Comedy that Make You **Funnier**, **Happier**, and **Better Looking**

The
ELEMENTS
of
HUMOR

WILEY

Published by John Wiley & Sons, Inc., Hoboken, New Jersey.
Published simultaneously in Canada.

For general information on our other products and services or for technical support, please contact our Customer Care Department within the United States at (800) 762-2974, outside the United States at (317) 572-3993 or fax (317) 572-4002.

Wiley also publishes its books in a variety of electronic formats. Some content that appears in print may not be available in electronic formats. For more information about Wiley products, visit our web site at www.wiley.com.

Library of Congress Cataloging-in-Publication Data

Names: Dikkers, Scott, author.
Title: The elements of humor : the tools of comedy that make you funnier, happier, and better looking / Scott Dikkers.
Description: First edition. | Hoboken, New Jersey : Wiley, 2024. | Includes bibliographical references and index.
Identifiers: LCCN 2024028317 (print) | LCCN 2024028318 (ebook) | ISBN 9781394269198 (Paperback) | ISBN 9781394269211 (adobe pdf) | ISBN 9781394269204 (epub)
Subjects: LCSH: Wit and humor—Handbooks, manuals, etc.
Classification: LCC P53.43 .D55 2024 (print) | LCC P53.43 (ebook) | DDC 398/.7—dc23/eng/20240805
LC record available at https://lccn.loc.gov/2024028317
LC ebook record available at https://lccn.loc.gov/2024028318

Cover Design: Paul McCarthy
Cover Art: © Steve Bloom Images / Alamy Stock Photo
SKY10087490_101024

Contents

Preface

I'm told some book aficionados enjoy prefaces. As for me, I skip past them. Forewords, too. Even dedications are a waste of my time. How does an author's message to "my sainted mother" or "my two beautiful children" improve the book-reading experience? I'm just trying to enjoy *Ready, Set, Prep: How to Build Your Doomsday Bunker*. I don't want to see a private love note. Take me straight to motion-sensor perimeter guns that shoot zombies' heads off. Also, tips for storing my dried squirrel meat.

Forewords have always struck me as stuffy. Just because Mr. Important endorses a book doesn't mean I have to like it. I can judge the contents of a book myself, thank you very much. If anything, forewords create unrealistic expectations. They set me up for disappointment. And I certainly don't care where or when you wrote it. Why are foreword writers compelled to share this irrelevant information? Ooh, you were in New York City on May 3, 2019? *Fancy!*

What's most troubling about a foreword is the not-so-subtle implication that I *have* to read it. It's like a threshold guardian in the front of the book, demanding I take this prerequisite test if I want to move forward. I don't like that pressure. It's passive-aggressive. The word *foreword* itself brings to mind a handsy suitor. Back off, forewords! I just want to read a book. I'm not interested in the literary equivalent of an unsolicited dick pic.

For those curious about the origins of a book, prefaces are the least annoying solution. What's the harm in some insight or background on why the author wrote the book? It's like a DVD commentary – optional, but there if you want it.

My earliest recollections of humor as a mode of communication began with Dr. Seuss. My mother read me *The Cat in the Hat, Horton Hears a Who*, and the rest of the Dr. Seuss canon in my earliest years. Seuss's wordplay, boundless imagination, and impossibly silly drawings opened a door to a fantastical world where I felt I belonged, unlike the real world. He was the gateway drug that lead to the harder stuff, *Sesame Street*. Jim Henson and company coaxed me further inside that world, introducing lovable characters whose funny flapping arms and corny jokes amazed and delighted me. As a fringe benefit, these early influences also taught me to read and write.

I understood why reading and writing were important. Every authority endorsed these skills. Humor, however, was not encouraged. In fact, every pillar of society considered it counterproductive. Don't be silly at the dinner table. Don't giggle at worship services. Don't crack wise in school. The message from every quarter was clear: humor is forbidden.

But I needed it. I was the scion of a long line of farmers, preachers, and puritans who believed meaning in life came not through joy or levity, but through suffering and hard work. I was lonely, withdrawn, and bullied. I was lost in my head most of the time, finding safety and comfort only in that other world.

I began to fight against the tide. I self-published my first work of humor, *Jokes and Riddles*, which I illustrated myself on scrap paper and stapled together into a book. I was four.

With this humble volume, I earned my first laugh. I took my first step into the comedy business, making important industry connections. Well, one connection. My grandma liked it. Her approval sparked something. It gave me the positive reinforcement I needed to continue working. I was like those famous stand-up comedians you hear about who go on stage for the first time, hear the laughter, and know immediately this is what they need to do for the rest of their lives.

Then, something happened that changed everything. The world of comedy as I knew it exploded as if from a Big Bang. I discovered *MAD* magazine. Apparently, nothing was sacred. Everything could be ridiculed – even my beloved Muppets!

Emboldened, I expanded my humor repertoire. I told funny stories and put on plays at home and at school. I became a class cutup. I drew cartoons. I did impressions. I juggled. I couldn't be stopped.

Why? What was it about humor that possessed me so powerfully and so completely?

Normal channels of communication, like making friends, making small talk, or playing sports, didn't come naturally to me. They existed outside the fantastical world and didn't make sense to me. Humor was how I interfaced with reality and connected with people. It was my ticket to the ride of life. It transformed me into Prometheus, gathering up whimsy from across the chasm and spreading this elixir of the gods like pixie dust over the world of the normals.

The
ELEMENTS
of
HUMOR

CHAPTER

1

The Unknowable

A mysterious force sneaks up and tickles us from time to time – often several times a day. It finds us when we least expect it. It comes at us from every direction: TV, computer, and phone screens; the people and events in our lives; casual conversations; random mishaps; our own heads, where it pops in unannounced while we take a shower or sit in traffic.

Like a visit from a mischievous pixie, it invades our thoughts with a ridiculous image or idea.

The devilish spirit always surprises. It's a sudden puff of pepper in our faces that makes us sneeze. Even when we seek it out, going to comedy clubs, watching funny movies, or reading satirical articles, it still somehow surprises. When it finds us, or we find it, we do its bidding. We respond on cue.

We laugh.

We suffer some kind of seizure, a healing spasm that takes over our bodies. Suddenly transformed into heated kernels, we explode into popcorn as if destined to achieve this enlightened state. Anyone nearby notices immediately and wants to know, "What's so funny?" Everyone wants in on this action. It's so contagious, people nearby – including strangers – start laughing before they even know what's funny.

But then, just as quickly as this sprite possesses us, it disappears without a trace.

What is this unknowable thing? Where does it come from? How is it generated? And why are we laughing at it?

We call it *humor*. And we need it. We need it the same way we need companionship, sunlight, clean air, and a good night's sleep. Sometimes it's our only weapon against life's trials, challenges, and misfortunes. Without humor, the world would lose all color.

Yet, despite its importance in our lives, nobody can seem to explain what humor is. It defies definition with the same slippery and unpredictable impishness that brings it to us. It's a trickster in the night with no name. It's a faceless echo in a maze of mirrors. Our best effort to explain it after it leaves us is hopelessly vague and ignorant: "I don't know – it was just funny."

Full-time masters of the craft of humor, who make millions of dollars whipping it up, are as tongue-tied as the rest of us. "I don't know," they say, throwing up their hands, "I just come up with funny things."

In recent decades, humor has been the subject of increasingly serious scientific study. Unfortunately, it falls far behind the study of every related category, including emotion, mental health, social behavior, relationships, and cognitive processes, but we'll take what we can get.

Love, for example, is a similarly powerful yet unseen force in the human experience. But that's where the similarity ends. The way we treat these two delightful aspects of life couldn't be more different. Love enjoys a depth and breadth of attention, fascination, and examination far in excess of humor. We write voluminous odes, songs, textbooks, poems, and stories about love. There are myriad counselors guiding us on how to get more of it and how to strengthen what we have of it. The state recognizes and codifies love with legal contracts, licenses, and laws. Love powers a $70-billion-a-year wedding industry.

Humor is the poor cousin, always left behind, in the boondocks, in a sketchy neighborhood, barely getting by. An infinitesimal fraction has been written about humor, comedy, and the funny arts. There are no comedy counselors. The state couldn't care less if we never laughed, and nobody gives out licenses for it. It does, however, make some money, though not nearly wedding-industry money. People all over the world pay for streaming services, comedy shows, books, magazines, nightclubs – and more – just trying to get a taste of it.

Laughter is the best medicine, so the saying goes. But if it's such effective medicine, why can't anyone describe how the medicine works? Why do we not have specific directions to the drug store where we can get it? Why is its manufacture a cryptic rite? Imagine a pharmaceutical company that doesn't know how to make penicillin or aspirin. That's us with humor. We leave it up to chance. We watch a sitcom, a silly movie, or a sketch, and sometimes we find it hilarious; other times, we're left disappointed. There are no guarantees in humor.

We seem determined to keep humor outside our conscious awareness, as if knowing too much about it will spoil it.

This book attempts to remedy, in a tiny way, the short shrift society has traditionally given to humor. And although I can't guarantee that if you consume the pages ahead you'll always know where to find it and your own attempts at it will always succeed, I can offer some collective wisdom that will at least help you appreciate humor when you catch it and make you more confident when you create it.

Failing this moonshot effort, *The Elements of Humor* nonetheless pursues the worthwhile goal of giving humor its due. It does this by providing a detailed framework for the concept of humor, with terms we can all use and categories we can all understand. It provides clear and specific instructions for whirling the mysterious particles that create humor, and in the process, demystifies the activity. Laid out in the chapters ahead are the best practices for bringing more humor into our lives and spreading it wherever we go, to brighten our days and the days of everyone around us.

The *How to Write Funny* series, my other books on the art and craft of humor, is a set of comprehensive, academic books intended to help the professional comedy writer compose better material. They're the equivalent of a scientific article on the subject in a journal only other scientists read.

This book takes a broader approach. It's for the layperson. It's for the nonprofessional as well as the would-be professional. It's for the hobbyist who wants more humor in the world. It's for the shy introvert who's afraid to say anything, let alone something funny. It's for the nervous hopeful trying to ask a crush for a date. It's for the corporate keynoter, toastmaster, and copywriter. It's for anyone who wants to get better at making people laugh. It's for anyone who believes that humor is important enough to take seriously.

For the humorist, it's a style guide. Just as Strunk and White's *The Elements of Style* is the essential guidebook for serious writers, showing them how to compose sentences with economy and pointing out where the commas should go, *The Elements of Humor* strives to be the essential guidebook for serious humorists, showing them how to use the tools of humor and pointing out where the punchlines should go. (Hint: they should go at the end.)

E. B. White, the White in Strunk and White, fittingly uttered the most famous statement about the perils of analyzing humor, a grim warning quoted (most often misquoted) by just about everyone who has ever attempted to explain the concept of humor: "Humor can be dissected, as a frog can," he said, "but the thing dies in the process and the innards are discouraging to any but the pure scientific mind." The quote comes from his short essay, "Some Remarks on Humor" (Harper Perennial, 2014), which serves as his resignation from the entire affair of explaining humor.

In it, he admits to finding humor "a complete mystery," something so fragile and evasive that it crumbles if anyone tries to explain it.

He gave up too easily. We live in a crowded and competitive world. The stakes have been raised since the days of *The Elements of Style*. White, resuscitating and embellishing a set of tips written by his departed former teacher William Strunk Jr., provided a durable manual for clear and concise writing, and by extension, speaking. Their book has been the leader in the field for nearly a century. *The Elements of Humor* takes their important work a step further. The population of the world has increased eightfold since *The Elements of Style* was first published, and the multitudes have more accessible platforms to write, speak, create audio and video entertainment and communication – and distribute it worldwide – than Strunk and White could have imagined. In this fast-moving, technologically driven attention economy, clear and concise communication is nice – a minimum, competent standard, to be sure – but it's no longer enough to rise above the din. With the added dimension of humor, communication not only gets its point across, it does it with razzle-dazzle. It attracts more attention, builds stronger rapport, and stays longer in people's memory.

How This Book Is Organized

The book will begin by describing concepts and behaviors that you already know and can easily replicate. These introductory sections will make the skill of humor seem so simple that you'll wonder why an entire book is necessary to articulate how it works.

As the chapters go on, however, the concepts will get increasingly challenging, always building on the more basic concepts that precede them. By improving your aptitude for humor this way, you'll always have one foot planted on familiar ground before you take any bold steps forward into new territory.

Go at your own pace. You don't need to master the exercises in each chapter before moving on to the next. You can try any of these exercises at any time and experience the same benefits.

Some books on humor provide canned jokes you can use. This book will provide no such jokes, at least not intentionally. Canned jokes might get a laugh and might make you feel funny, but let's set a higher standard. Canned jokes are unnatural, inauthentic, and more sad than funny. The best humor stems from who you are. It works best when it's original, spontaneous, and accentuates your personality. Therefore, we'll spend some time getting you acquainted with yourself to find your comedy persona.

Real humor creates rapport between people. Canned humor creates distance.

The chapters ahead will offer many suggestions and examples, always with the intent to cultivate your innate sense of humor, something you can draw on effortlessly in any situation, conversation, or medium of entertainment.

Best Practices

- Use humor to elevate your communication to a new, impactful level.

- Produce, enjoy, and understand humor with the confidence that it's a legitimate and productive pursuit, despite its reputation for being frivolous.

- Don't use canned jokes.

Exercises

1. Look at the role of humor in your life. How do you get it? Where do you get it? How much of it do you create yourself?
2. Next time you laugh, allow yourself to take a moment afterwards to assess what made you laugh, and why.

2

What Is Humor?

Humans have been making each other laugh since before we emerged in Africa a quarter million years ago. We developed a fun new communication skill that induced laughter, smoothed over conflict, tightened social bonds, and made life more enjoyable. Other humanoid species probably used humor, too. Neanderthals are known to have been capable of symbolic thought. They made tools, ritually buried their dead, and used pigments, possibly to decorate themselves or their clothing. Like us, they probably thought butts were funny, too.

How deep does the proto-human predilection for humor go?

Humor in Animals

Further back through the evolutionary tree, you can't find a group of creatures funnier than chimps. Jane Goodall often observed chimps laughing in her groundbreaking work. Erica Cartmill, an anthropology professor at Indiana University, confirmed in lab studies that bonobos and orangutans laugh and play tricks on each other.

Even further down the tree, we notice dogs. None other than Charles Darwin believed our best friends capable of humor distinct from play, writing in 1871 what every dog owner already knows:

> … if a bit of stick or other such object be thrown to one, he will often carry it away for a short distance; and then squatting down with it on the ground close before him, will wait until his master comes quite close to take it away. The dog will then seize it and rush away in triumph, repeating the same maneuver, and evidently enjoying the practical joke.

More distant mammalian relatives experience humor, too. Dr. Jaak Panksepp of Bowling Green State University and Dr. Jeffrey Burgdorf of Northwestern University learned this fact by tickling a lot of rats. Turns out, rats can laugh.

Humor in Babies

Bolstering the idea that humor is baked into our DNA, Gabriella Airenti, a psychology professor at the University of Turin, found that children under the age of five understand humorous, nonverbal games and other nonliteral jokes at a much earlier age than scientists previously thought. In her studies, children as young as 10 months grasped concepts like irony and intentional deception followed by gestures indicating the classic rejoinder "just kidding." Babies grasp this type of communication even before they develop the ability to interpret the thoughts, feelings, and intentions of others. Laughter starts appearing even earlier, at four months.

Babies and toddlers react knowingly when, for example, they hold out a toy to someone and then yank it away at the last moment, frustrating the other person's attempt to grab it. Cartmill's apes enjoyed the same shenanigans when they teased each other with bananas. Darwin's dog played the same game.

The Universal Field Theory of Humor

These rudimentary activities reveal a set-up/punchline structure: offer the object, take it away. No less an expert than any scientist, George Carlin, said, "Comedy always leads you down one direction and then grabs you and pulls you in the other direction." It's what professor Peter McGraw, the director of the Humor Research Lab at the University of Colorado–Boulder, calls a *benign violation*. He says the source of all humor is a violation (like withholding a banana), but one that's mostly harmless.

In his book *The Humor Code*, McGraw lays out this universal field theory of humor. It provides insight into what humor is: trouble without harm. Mischief without lawbreaking. Humor can make people die laughing without actually killing them.

You can see the results of this successful formula in the face of a baby playing peekaboo. In this elemental form of humor – probably the first humor we all experience – someone familiar disappears and then reappears. A violation, then a surprise reveal that the violation is benign. It's a simple trick, like teasing with a banana or stick. What makes the unwitting audience laugh is the confirmation that nothing dangerous has happened. (Throughout this book, for the sake of simplicity, I'll refer to anyone on the receiving end of humor as the *audience*, and anyone on the delivering end, the *humorist*.)

Humor Across Cultures

Given all the babies and animals who've been subjected to teasing, tickling, and outright banana theft, we can see that humor is an instinct we all share. But is it universal? Is it possible for humor to bridge language and cultural barriers?

Since the African Exodus some 60,000 to 70,000 years ago, societies around the world have developed humor differently. Just as religion, fashion, and custom diverged, so did attitudes and customs regarding humor. In the past few hundred years, unfortunate stereotypes have tarred some peoples around the world as being less inclined to humor. If someone looks different from us, we can develop the prejudice that these "strangers" or "enemies" aren't as fully human as we are.

The enlightened reality is that we all have the same ability to create and enjoy humor. Different cultures merely emphasize it in different ways. New studies show that although wildly disparate cultures such as East and West show differences in how humor is perceived, *at* the source of these differences is not incompetence, but anxiety. Tonglin Jiang, a psychology professor at the University of Hong Kong, found that the greatest differences in humor between Eastern and Western cultures had more to do with people feeling insecure about their ability to wield humor rather than any innate lack of talent.

Proficiency with humor is in our blood. The tools outlined in this book stem from this shared inheritance. They work to create humor with any age group and in any part of the world. The simplest of these tools might even work on a chimp, dog, or rat.

The Lost Skill of Humor

Humor is universal. It's our birthright, no different than the yellow warbler's birthright to sing its sweet song. But if this is the case, why do so many people struggle to communicate successfully with humor? Why is everyone not a master comedian?

The answer to this riddle can be found in the paradigm-shifting theories of British zoologist Desmond Morris. He realized that modern humans, living in our specialized civilization, are cut off from the habitat where we evolved and became human, where our forebears lived in tightly knit, family-based tribes of about 500 people living a hunter-gatherer existence. Nested in this evolutionary comfort zone on the African Savanna, we developed all our signature human skills and traits in order to survive and thrive.

Today, we're not living in social structures that anyone in our ancient evolutionary history would describe as "normal" or "natural." Our modern way of life would be unrecognizable – even unthinkable – to our ancestors. We're not hunting or gathering. We're not warring with other tribes. We're not escaping from predators. Instead, we're either isolated or mired in artificial environments like public schools, offices, big cities, and daily commutes. We're punching in, sitting in cubicles, going to happy hour, and staring at screens. We're wading through cesspools of competition with strangers and perceived enemies, conflicts we don't know how to resolve. We rarely have the opportunity to summon the instincts we forged over countless generations to do anything they were meant to do.

We've adapted to our new way of living, but not without a price. We're so far outside our natural habitat that many of the traits that faithfully served our species for millennia have fallen into disuse. Worse, some are now harmful. Traits, for example, like our penchant for instant gratification, our love of sweets, and our inability to see slow-moving threats, are the source of modern problems like addiction, mental illness, and obesity. Our fight-or-flight stress response fires almost continuously. We yell in traffic. We abuse each other. We collect the stress in our bodies and become wracked with back pain, joint pain, skin problems, and so on.

We are, Morris argues, animals in a zoo, pulled from our evolutionary environment. We suffer the same distress and changes in biological pathways seen in caged animals. In short, we've gone insane. And insane people have more important things to worry about than trying to be funny. Humor was necessary in our evolutionary development, but it's not necessary now. In a complex, modern society choked with anxiety, making jokes is a frivolous luxury. As a result, the skill has atrophied in many of us.

Yellow warblers, however, inhabit the trees and skies like they always have, and they need to sing to survive. If they don't develop their singing skills to the best of their ability, they can't compete, reproduce, or thrive.

One of the many differences between us and the yellow warbler is that we're not driven in the way our forebears were, whether by the necessities of survival, social cohesion, or sexual selection, to develop our instinct for humor to the highest possible degree. Most of us aren't competing in the human equivalent of the cut-throat, Darwinian jungle (that is, suburban backyards) where the yellow warbler plies its song. We're plodding through modern life like inmates in an urban prison, just cogs in a machine.

The Hope of Humor

Some humans, though not many, have rediscovered their instinct for humor and chosen to nurture it to its fullest potential. The particular circumstances of their lives, for one reason or another, made humor necessary. Maybe it was a way to get parental attention. Maybe it was their need for distinction among peers. Their paths might be different, but their drive is the same. Just like the yellow warbler needs to develop the best song, these humorists need to develop the best sense of humor. They need this skill to compete in the evolutionary arms race. They learn early in life, probably subconsciously, that humor is a shield they can use to protect themselves, an olive branch they can use to defuse conflict and bond with others, a salve they can use to relieve stress, and an art they can use to woo a mate.

These are the funniest people you know: the office cutups, the successful comedians, and the professional humor writers.

The question is, how can you reclaim your birthright and rediscover your innate ability to make people laugh?

Best Practices

- You have an instinct for humor, and you're entitled to use it.
- Create humor like you would in a game of peekaboo with a baby, executed to varying degrees of complexity.

Exercises

1. Remember instances when you did or said things that others perceived as funny. Revel in those experiences.
2. What are the most stressful things in your life? Think of ways you can reframe them with humor.

CHAPTER

3

Quick Start

Perfect pitch is a rare gift. If you picked 10,000 random people, at most only five would have it. Someone with perfect pitch can identify any note of the scale on command without a reference pitch or the help of an instrument. Ask a singer blessed with this gift to give you a C# and they'll pluck it out of thin air with the same ease the rest of us recall a common vocabulary word.

Because most people – even most professional singers – don't have perfect pitch, when an acapella group begins singing on stage, someone has to first play a note on a kazoo. This "pitch pipe" orients the singers to the correct starting note, guiding them to begin their song in the right key.

Most humorists need a pitch pipe, too. Before you use humor in any medium – writing, performing, or others – you need to set the tone, not just for yourself but for your audience. Whether the audience is a single person sitting across from you at a diner or thousands of screaming fans at Madison Square Garden, they need to be properly primed to receive and process your humor. All humor is performative, to varying degrees. Therefore, the onus is on the humorist to set the stage for any attempt at being funny.

The Tone of Humor

One of the central questions that's traditionally dogged those who've tried to explain humor or produce it on command is, where does humor come from? The answer is not a mystery. When we were children, we all played and needed very little impetus to do so. We lived to play. As adults, many of us have closed off this particular avenue of enjoyment. But the desire is still there. By simply tapping into the sense of childlike play we've likely buried, we can reignite our desire to have childlike fun.

The right tone can be conveyed in all the usual ways we communicate with each other: verbally, textually, symbolically, and physically. Humor manifests in various tones, each influenced by factors such as the humorist's disposition, the audience's receptivity, and the context or location of the interaction (see Chapter 6). Although these tones can vary widely, they all share a common denominator:

playtime. Regardless of the situation, the humorist's job is to gamify communication.

Three easy ways to set the tone for humor:

- Smile
- Laugh
- Make a nonthreatening gesture like any variation of palms up or open palms

When done well, communicating with humor puts people at ease, it shows them they're part of a friendly interaction, it helps them remember the message and the messenger, and it brings them closer together.

Communication Plus

Humor, at its core, is communication. Most of us already know how to communicate, but perhaps some of us feel too awkward to approach it with a sense of humor. After all, who has time for nonsense? We're adults, and we have important information to exchange.

Using everyday conversation as a jumping-off point, it can be helpful to think of humor as simply a more playful conversation, or normal communication with a little extra fun thrown in.

Clear and competent communication without humor happens all the time: in courtrooms when lawyers lay out evidence, in business emails with clients and colleagues, and when we explain our issue to tech support.

Purely informational exchanges like these require less effort than communicating with humor. The humorist brings something more to the table: a dessert to round out the main course of thoughts, stories, and opinions that might otherwise be communicated plainly. Potentially hard-to-swallow, humorless communication is refreshed with the rich and flavorful icing of a few laughs. When we add humor, we communicate ideas just as meaningfully as before, but with more enjoyment for everyone involved.

A sense of playfulness in communication can come disguised in many forms. This is part of the fun – the peekaboo element. For example, those who convey humor in a serious tone can create humor out of the contrast between delivery and material. Some people can be funny when they're sad, sharing their sob stories with humor, partly to soothe themselves, partly to make their misery palatable to their audience. We'll explore these tones and others in later chapters.

Being Aware

We all need to be aware of the person or persons we're communicating with to say the right thing and avoid miscommunication. Humor has earned a reputation in recent years for being an incendiary activity. The humorist, we're told, needs to be extra careful, lest a bad joke offend someone.

Being funny at the wrong time, too soon, or "inappropriately" are faux pas no humorist wants to commit. Anyone out of practice in the skill of humor risks being tone deaf to such missteps. But non-humorous communicators suffer the same fate just as often – if not more often – than humorists. Not all communication is welcome. Words can offend when they're communicated flatly just as easily – if not more easily – as when they're communicated humorously.

Humor is subjective, but not entirely so. There are many ways you can manage people's expectations and make your humor more objectively funny. One way is to notice the mood of those around you. Assess whether anyone is interested in your humorous take. Being conscious of people's state before you say something to them is a good policy in general. Some people don't want to be approached or addressed. Ignoring their cues and talking anyway can be rude. Being conscious of people's state before you say something funny is a good policy, too. The difference is that talking to people with humor serves as an ice-breaker. It's more often welcomed, regardless of the initial level of interest.

The humorist also needs to be aware of the political dynamics in a group. Jokes told to a bunch of friends will land much differently than the same jokes told to your boss at a board meeting. Humor is less about you than the people you're hoping to amuse. Put yourself in their shoes. What are they thinking about? What are their struggles? Your humor will succeed more often when you relate to people, match their energy, and meet them where they are.

Thinking Differently

All of us have millions of shared experiences and similar thought patterns in common. As humans, we're more alike than different. What makes you different is your perspective on the similarities. We all wear masks, try to blend in, and communicate like everyone else. To be yourself, you have to avoid these impulses, avoid the groupthink that's influenced you in the past, let go of the urge to conform once in a while, and communicate in a way that only you can. You do this by being yourself.

Humor is about originality. Think about things you don't usually think about. Interrupt your thought patterns and the thought patterns of the people in your circle. Try to say something genuine to you, something you've never heard anyone say before. Try to connect it to how you're feeling. You might be surprised to find humor quickly with this simple practice.

Sometimes silly, random things are funny. You'll see how this works in Chapter 16. For now, experiment. Introduce out-of-place topics and ideas that don't belong.

Embracing Failure

It's important to realize no serious harm will come of you trying to do something funny and failing. Humor is not fire rescue, and it's not an exact science either. The best we can hope for is an improved batting average. And adopting a willingness to fail is one of the best ways to improve your batting average.

Failing at being funny is, traditionally, one of our gravest embarrassments. We're especially afraid of bombing on stage. However, any successful comedian will tell you bombing early and often is essential. It builds confidence. Comedians need to bomb in order to learn their craft. And they all have funny stories about the times they bombed the worst.

The stakes are lower than you think. No one will excommunicate you from humanity if you try to be funny and fall short. You're not going to be banished from the community. The only damage will be to your ego, and such damage is good for you. Try, fail, and don't sweat it. Failing is the first step of learning a new skill.

You'll learn techniques in Chapter 19 to turn the embarrassment of failure into an advantage that will make you funnier.

A Relaxed State

We all have some level of performance anxiety when it comes to humor. You can mitigate this anxiety by reframing your nervousness. When our audience doesn't get a joke, it makes us tense up. We sweat. It's painful. Rest assured, it's happened to all of us, from the big-money, professional comedian to the fledgling class clown. No matter who you are, it feels terrible.

To deliver humor successfully, you need to be relaxed. One way to avoid tensing up from anxiety is to remember what it's like to play peekaboo with a baby. Do you feel anxious that a baby won't get your joke? Chances are, you don't. You're probably more amused than anxious. This is the proper mindset to approach any attempt at humor, regardless of the complexity of the humor or the age of your audience.

If you're nervous being funny because you don't think you're funny, change your inner script. Saying "I'm not funny" or "I don't have a good sense of humor" is like saying "I didn't enjoy playing as a child." It's like a bird saying "I can't fly." Instead, tell yourself, "I allow myself to be funny" and "I have a wonderful sense of humor."

Best Practices

- Before you use humor, set the tone for yourself and your audience.
- To create humor, play.
- Communicate, but with an added layer of fun.
- Relate to people, match their energy, and meet them where they are.
- Be yourself.
- Allow yourself to make mistakes. Enjoy the process.
- If you fall into negative self-talk or suffer anxiety about humor, tell yourself you have a wonderful sense of humor.

Exercises

1. Do something childish alone in the comfort of your own home.
2. Find a buddy or a group of friends to be silly with. Enjoy some laughs.

4

The Humor Mindset

Hot-rodders have a gizmo that pumps nitrous oxide into their gas tanks. If they're traveling at high speed, flipping the nitrous switch will make them go even faster, giving them the real-world version of the "turbo boost" depicted in Batman cartoons and outer-space movies.

Humor is like nitrous oxide injected into a conversation. A verbal exchange traveling at normal high speed, with its logical statement-making and information sharing, gets an intellectual and emotional lift when humor takes it to a new plateau. Everyone involved is suddenly aware of how witty the conversation has become. Although there are variants in our intelligence levels, even the average and below average can use the tools of humor to give their communication this power surge.

This chapter lists a few specific guideposts along the speedway of a conversation or presentation charged with a burst of humor.

A Clown State of Mind

For a critical period in childhood, we said whatever came to our minds. How the people around us reacted to this set our brains firmly on one of two tracks.

If the people around us laughed with us and enjoyed our banter, we became easy with humor, happy to try to do or say funny things, fail sometimes, succeed other times, and possibly not care to improve or think of humor as a skill that needed development.

If the people around us didn't respond much, or told us to be quiet too many times, we likely went down the other path, the path of fear. Saying or doing anything funny became risky. The lack of encouragement we got from our surroundings stifled us, and we self-censored.

If you're an example of the latter, people probably call you shy, quiet, or mousy. They might even say you have no sense of humor. You can use the exercises in this book to regain your playful spirit.

If you're an example of the former, people probably call you fun, silly, possibly a blabbermouth, or "always on." You can use the exercises in this book to refine your chatter into more precision efforts at being funny.

In order for your mind to be fertile ground for humor, thinking of the creative brain as having two halves can be helpful. One half is a clown. The other half is an editor. Think of them as the right and left sides of your brain. The science of left and right brain has been largely discredited in recent years, but it's a useful framework to understand humor.

Think of the right side of your brain as the crazy, fun half. It wants to be creative. It wants to say whatever it thinks, with no filter. It's the three-year-old in you. This is the clown brain.

Think of the left side of your brain as the disciplinarian, the librarian who wants you to shush. It's the picky, skeptical part of you that judges everything you say before you say it. This is the editor brain.

Most of us are stuck in editor brain, cripplingly nervous to let our clown side shine. We're programmed to be buttoned-up adults. This programming is so strong, we poo-poo childish things like being silly and having fun. A far smaller number of us lean toward clown brain. One of the reasons we love comedians and comedy writers is that they're allowed to break past their editor and have fun being a clown.

SERIOUSLY?

An Editor State of Mind

Most of us favor the editor side of our brain so heavily that the clown side of our brains has atrophied. This is you if you're afraid to be funny, if you stop yourself before you put voice to a funny thought, or if you don't think it's appropriate to do or say silly things. You're really ossified if you say things like "I could never do that," or "I'm just not capable of being funny."

As we age, we lean toward the editor. We learn that to exist in polite society, we need to stop being foolish. We need to grow up. It's important to realize that adulthood is merely a mask we wear to get through our lives without making waves and without embarrassing ourselves.

On *Monty Python's Flying Circus*, one of Graham Chapman's most beloved characters was a colonel who broke up sketches, demanding the group put a stop to all the silliness. He's a funny and accurate depiction of the editor brain. Other examples of the editor:

- A parent saying "shush" in a worship service
- A teacher admonishing you for giggling, doodling, or joking around in class
- A supervisor who demands you stop horsing around and get back to work

A constant correction of your "childish" behavior compounds in your life to make you someone who thinks being funny is wrong. You've been conditioned to think it's not mature behavior.

It's true that humorous behavior is not usually mature, and that's exactly why it's so fun. Being a straitlaced adult is boring. Being a child is a blast.

You probably already say silly things to your best friend. You feel safe with that person. A lot of us feel our funniest when we're around our closest friends. This is where we allow our most childlike selves to come out and play.

Funny people, funny writers, and comedians feel safe showing that part of themselves in a more expansive circle. They do it with acquaintances, strangers, and large audiences.

In order to use humor more effectively, you need to expand your circle.

Just Kidding

Like peekaboo, humor is often a momentary dip into a funhouse mirror reflecting back at us. We show the people around us a different way of seeing things, and we hope they'll find it funny. Then, just as quickly as we make the joke, there's an expected "just kidding" moment that follows. This is the moment when you reassure the audience that the funhouse mirror image is not reality. The idea can be expressed in a few different ways, with each way identifying the joke as a benign violation.

In more sophisticated humor, the "just kidding" message is silent. The audience figures it out on their own. If you find you have to say "just kidding" too often in order for people to get your humor, you either need to employ the tools of humor more skillfully or you need to reassess how much droll, deadpan humor your audience can handle.

When Humor Doesn't Work

Humor often produces unforeseen difficulties. If you play a game of peekaboo with a baby who doesn't know you, you might be met with a confused stare, or worse, a sudden meltdown – the baby equivalent of booing and heckling.

Any time humor doesn't work is an opportunity to learn. If you can calm yourself, wipe off your flop sweat, and regain your composure, you can think through why a humor attempt didn't work, and you can try something else.

As our humor gets more sophisticated, we experience a more complex set of emotional responses when our attempts at humor don't succeed. If an audience of adults doesn't laugh, we suddenly feel rejected, like we're a failure at life.

The easiest way to manage these feelings is to remember the peekaboo experience. How did you react when your joke didn't land with the baby? You laughed it off. You felt bad for the baby. You didn't take it personally. You didn't feel slighted by the baby. You didn't suddenly start questioning your self-worth.

Using the peekaboo game as a reference point enables you to play the role of the unquestioned adult in the situation. To get good at humor, you need to act like the adult, at least in terms of your emotional response to failure. (Rest assured, you're best served acting like an irresponsible child when it comes to humor.)

"Failure" in humor is just a misunderstanding. It's not a judgment cast against you. It doesn't mean you're a terrible person. It just means you've done something we've all done: you tried to be funny and failed. Laugh it off. Have some sympathy for the audience instead of yourself. After all, they just had to listen to a bad joke. Apologize if you feel you did something that offended, and take advantage of the learning opportunity.

Best Practices

- Think of your brain as having two halves, a clown and an editor. Try not to favor one over the other.
- Humor is always followed by a "just kidding" moment, spoken or unspoken, to ensure the audience understands the joke.
- When your attempt at humor fails, instead of taking it personally, take the opportunity to learn what went wrong and strive to improve.

Exercises

If you're stuck in editor brain:

1. Write a funny letter, opinion, or rant. Spend no more than 30 minutes. Don't edit it too heavily or try to make it perfect. It should tickle your funny bone and it should not be hard.
2. Try saying something funny to someone other than a close friend. You pick the person. Say it with a smile.

If you're stuck in clown brain:

1. Write something funny and then get some feedback from a friend who has some writing experience. If you don't have such a friend, join the Writers Room, a feedback group I run with the How to Write Funny community. Spend 30 minutes reworking the writing and implementing the feedback you got.

2. Write down some of the funny things you said in the last week. Make two columns: one for the hits, one for the misses.

5

The Right Kind of Laughs

Are people laughing with you or at you?

You might be surprised to learn that professional comedians don't care what kind of laughs they get. Laughs are laughs, and they're happy to get them any way they can. Experienced comedians are practiced at playing the fool. They display undesirable behavior ranging from stupidity to slovenliness to hyper-fixation, and they expect audiences not only to laugh at them but also to relate to these common foibles. Skilled humorists craft material that makes them the butt of the joke, inviting the audience to feel better about themselves. When we see how laughable they are, we're delighted to know at least we're not *that* bad. It's a rare successful comedian who stands on a pedestal, striving to look cool. Audiences can't relax or enjoy a comedian who's trying too hard to be better than they are. They prefer comedians and humorists to be "less than." They prefer to laugh *at*.

Of course, the dark side of being laughed at is verbal bullying. This kind of laughter can be traumatizing, especially when we're young. Such instances of laughter don't qualify as humor for our purposes, and they're outside the scope of this book. Don't be a bully.

As an adult, is it so bad to be the butt of a joke? Imagine good-natured teasing among friends. Imagine your kids laughing at how out of touch you are. This is the kind of "laughing at instead of with" we're aiming for.

There's a commonly held belief that laughter itself is a submissive gesture, that to laugh at someone is akin to a chimp bowing, huffing, and baring its teeth at a higher-status alpha chimp. When we laugh at someone, are we placing ourselves in a submissive or dominant position?

If someone is trying to make us laugh, and we're laughing, we acknowledge that they're more clever, and we want to bond with them. In this way, we're indeed making the chimp gesture of submission. By the same token, the humorist is tricking us with a complicated variant of peekaboo: "You thought I was in the dominant position, but look – I'm playing the fool. I'm actually in the submissive position." It's a dance where sometimes one partner leads, sometimes the other leads. The music that accompanies this dance is genuine rapport between audience and humorist.

Learn to enjoy yourself when people laugh at you. It might make you uncomfortable at first, but it will also make you a better humorist.

A Willingness to Try

To brave the indignity of being laughed at, you have to make the attempt. It's this daring to try where all humor is born. It's the brave first step you take to create the fun atmosphere. When you attempt humor, you also make an attempt to connect with people, find common ground with them, and make friends.

The best humorists, whether casual conversationalists or skilled professionals, make many attempts at humor. Their consistent attitude is that each attempt at humor is a brick laid over water to make a bridge. If they're met with confused looks, groans, or no laughter, they resist the impulse to frame the reaction as a personal rejection. Instead, they frame it as a learning experience: apparently that brick won't work for this bridge. They go back to the brick pile and find another that might work better.

An unskilled humorist might give up, or might keep trying with a scattershot approach, desperately and nervously saying anything that comes to mind – even canned jokes – hoping anything they say will be perceived as funny.

Using the funny filters (Chapter 8) can help you narrow the spread, with humor that will more likely than not hit the target.

Being Self-Effacing

Having confidence, as noted in Chapter 3 (and expounded on in Chapter 6), is an important prerequisite to creating successful humor. The idea of making fun of yourself may strike you as contradictory to having confidence. In fact, laughing at oneself is one of the most confident things a humorist can do. It's a charismatic quality. Trust it.

A wellspring of self-effacing humor can come from a willingness to play the boob, the klutz, or the forgetful, incompetent, or absent-minded idiot. Under normal circumstances, we're understandably desperate to avoid coming across as possessing any of these terrible qualities. But in the pursuit of humor, being willing to make fun of your own failings, temporarily playacting the weak, unintelligent, or ineffectual person, indicates to others that you're extremely confident.

The humorous person enjoys appearing "less than" in order to make other people feel superior, and to make them laugh. This is a concept called *dropping*. Characters in sketch and drama drop into base archetypes to create humor (see Chapter 10).

There's a fine line between self-effacing humor and humor that strikes people as self-hating. You don't want to make jokes that reveal deeper self-esteem problems that seep out from underneath a humorous facade. People won't know how to respond if, for example, you're claiming to be a loser who can't do anything right. You'll find the best success balancing a self-effacing attitude with relatable aspirations and honest self-knowledge.

Braving some of these foundational mindsets will be crucial for you to move forward and start generating humor in any medium, at whatever level you hope to achieve.

The Skill of Getting Laughs

If you think of yourself as someone who's awkward and unfunny, don't make the mistake of believing you're doomed to remain in this perceived state. Humor, like any endeavor in life, is a skill that can be learned. You just have to practice. The same as you would learn any new skill – from a sport to a musical instrument to Civil War reenacting – the practice in itself should be fun.

The idea that humor is an innate skill that can't be learned, that you have to be born funny, has been repeated so many times that most of us accept it as fact. It is a myth. The truth is the opposite. Everyone is funny. Many of us just haven't developed the skill. Maybe we don't need to. Maybe we don't want to. Maybe we never had the opportunity.

If you struggle with humor, remember that you've laughed plenty. You've joked around. You've written, said, or done things in your life that other people perceived as funny. You have a spectacular sense of humor like no one else's. It's as unique as your fingerprint.

You were born with the capacity to spout hilarious witticisms, tell funny stories, and delight everyone around you with jokes you think of on the spot. Your ability to be funny has the potential to be as beautiful and frequent as birdsong. All you need to do is embrace it.

Maybe you've experimented with creating humor in some form or other in the past and had a bad reaction. Maybe you thought it was funny but no one else did. Maybe you got discouraged. Maybe people didn't get your jokes. Maybe people thought you were being weird. Maybe someone got offended or upset. Maybe, in response to such bad experiences, you became gun-shy. Maybe you experienced this kind of reaction more than once early in life.

For whatever reason, if you haven't developed the skill of humor to the extent you'd like, that doesn't mean you don't have an incredible, innate ability.

As with any skill, before you master it, you lack nuance. You blunder and you make wide swings, mostly misses. This is normal. When babies learn to walk, they stumble and fall time after time. Only through repeated trying and failing do they learn this skill that will soon become second nature. No baby ever stood up and strolled across the floor like a boss on the first try.

Learning humor is no different. Be prepared to stumble around for a time. Count all your previous stumblings as notches on a wall, credits toward an eventual passing grade.

Social Lubricant

When we understand that the primary role of humor is to build rapport, this knowledge can help take the pressure off. There's no reason to feel performance anxiety. Even if you're a comedian on a comedy club stage, when you use humor, you're just talking to people.

Knowing when and how to joke around with someone is a skill that can take you far in life. You can use it to diffuse tension, smooth over awkwardness, make friends, and get ahead at work. Your humor can make people like you.

The best way to become adept at humor is to start with friends and loved ones. Let them know in advance that you're trying to develop your sense of humor and that they should expect you to joke around with them more often.

Be sure to ask them to let you know if your humor is coming off as mean or mocking. Always endeavor to use your humor to elevate them or tease yourself, rarely the other way around (unless you're adept at using irony, discussed in Chapter 9).

When you're comfortable after some practice with people you know, try kidding with strangers or acquaintances. If they at least smile, you know you're doing something right.

Work your way up to kidding around in high-stakes relationships like those with prospective colleagues or dinner dates.

When you find your groove with kidding, conversations will be more fun.

Kidding is usually an ice breaker, not a sustained mode of communicating. You kid once or twice, and then stop, transitioning smoothly to other types of humor or transitioning smoothly to more substantive or emotionally engaging conversation. Someone who's always kidding can be insufferable.

A Temporary Reality

As suggested in Chapter 4, a humorist often creates a temporary world in the telling of a joke or funny concept. In this world, one key thing is askew – either slightly or dramatically – from the real world. In peekaboo, it's a world where the humorist's face has disappeared. When the humor works, this single incongruity, the thing that makes this new world different, is funny.

For example, if you jokingly tell a coworker you're late because you couldn't find your briefcase, that's not funny because it's no different from the real world. If you say you're late because you couldn't find your shoehorn or because you live in a boxcar and woke up in Omaha, those are more ridiculous reasons to be late, and each creates a temporary reality in which those obviously false things are taken as true, at least until the "just kidding" moment kicks in.

Riffing

Most humorous comments can be expanded and made part of a conversation where the temporary world is extended. In a comedy writers room, this is called *riffing*. In improv, it's called *yes-anding*.

In conversation, if a person you're talking to is adept at humor and tells a joke, you can "yes and" their joke by accepting the temporary world of their joke and then making a joke in the same vein. You do this by asking yourself, if what they said is true, what else could be true? For example, if they say, "The rain is really coming down today. God wants Noah to go for it again," you would accept as reality that this rain is biblical in proportion by saying something like, "Was that the voice I heard this morning, telling me to gather two of every kind?"

This form of conversational joking also applies to written essays, articles, and performed monologues. A writer or performer needs to riff on a comedy take to find new jokes that build on each other to expand on the initial concept and build out the humorous, askew world.

Being Conscious of Your Target

Who or what you're making jokes about matters. Utilizing inanimate objects, locations, time periods, or ideas is generally a rich target environment, unless they're controversial or tragic.

The most common target in all humor is people and the things they do. In casual conversation, it can be easy to use humor as a weapon to target others with everything from a good-natured ribbing to mean-spirited ridicule. Targeting others can be a minefield and quickly turn sour. Even non-injurious, playful banter, whether with people you're talking to, people in view, or people who aren't in the vicinity and therefore incapable of defending themselves, can be perceived as cruel, and likely won't be funny.

If humor is loving and supportive, even if based in good-natured teasing, most people will find it acceptable. But if it's too harsh or too negative, the attempt at humor will reflect poorly on the humorist.

A key formula to remember when creating humor is "comfort the afflicted and afflict the comfortable." Due to your own unconscious biases, your humor will likely be perceived as mean-spirited unless you adopt this humor policy. Use your humor to raise people up, not tear them down. You can, however, tear down the powerful. People love seeing authority brought down a peg.

A Rich Humor Environment

We've seen that humor is a dimension of language, a tone, and an attitude. In the comedy business we talk in terms of whether something is funny or whether it gets laughs. Before these ultimate goals of humor can be achieved, the humorist must create the proper environment for humor. When an audience understands that humor is taking place, they're far more likely to respond positively to it. Creating this context is the responsibility of the humorist.

Sometimes humor itself can create the environment, one where people may not have realized humor existed until you or someone else introduced it. This is the power of humor: to elevate conversations and situations to be more entertaining.

The most critical ingredient in creating this environment is not the humorous joke, message, or comment. It's the messenger.

Best Practices

- Being laughed at and laughed with are both acceptable.
- Make fun of yourself.
- Consider each attempt at humor an effort to connect with others.
- A humorist creates a skewed reality and invites the audience to enjoy it.
- The most widely acceptable humor comforts the afflicted and afflicts the comfortable.

Exercises

1. Say something funny to someone other than a close friend. Say it with a smile, and remember to comfort the afflicted and afflict the comfortable.
2. Do something silly and unexpected while walking down the street or in a crowded area. Focus on making fun of yourself and being laughed at.

CHAPTER

6

Being in the Moment

To succeed with humor, you must know and be yourself. Your best humor will spring from you being you. For some, this kind of self-knowledge and self-direction might be easy. For others, it might open an existential wormhole. How can we truly know ourselves? Steve Martin, the most popular stand-up comedian of all time, said, "Who knows who their self is? I don't." Most comedians, in fact, take years to discover who they are and find their unique comic voice.

The good news is, you don't need to know the entirety of yourself to create humor. You don't need to know your deepest dreams, shadow self, or soul. You only need to know what people think of you.

An easy way to arrive at this paradigm-shifting information is to focus not on yourself, but on others. How do people perceive you? What have they said about you? Is there any part of you they've observed that you can accentuate for humor? Do you have any identifiable traits you can latch onto that align with a popular character archetype? (See Chapter 10.)

The character of the humorist is one of the most important ingredients in the recipe for humor. As the humor's delivery medium, whether you're presenting your own material or reciting someone else's, you – the medium – can't help but affect the message. It's the Heisenberg uncertainty principle of humor. The source of the joke alters the joke itself. A joke told by one person might be funny, yet when told by a different person, might bomb.

What is the difference? There are a few.

Confidence

Confidence can make almost anything funny. Finding confidence is easier said than done, of course. People spend their lives searching for it. There are entire volumes, online courses, and YouTube motivation videos set to Hans Zimmer music dedicated to the subject. (Charlie Houpert's *Charisma on Command* is a particularly helpful resource.)

The good news is that superhero confidence is essential only for the professional stand-up comedian. For the amateur humorist, writer, or someone merely hoping to improve their dexterity with conversational humor, a mortal-human level of confidence is adequate.

If you're shy, reserved, or don't think of yourself as a confident person, you can rewrite that script. Confidence can always be generated through the "fake it 'til you make it" approach. Pretending to be confident is, in fact, the best way to achieve real confidence.

One way to practice faking it is to ask yourself, "Has there been a time in my life when I've felt confident?" Remember that time. What was happening? What made you feel confident? Re-create that feeling when you need it. Stand like you stood then. Hold your body and head like you did then. Breathe like you did then. Make a face like you did then. Speak like you did then.

If you feel like you have no justification to be confident, remember that it's not the circumstances of our lives that make us confident, it's the stories (or lies) we tell ourselves about the circumstances of our lives. It's easy to say, "I was confident that day because I told off Mr. Buckner to his face." But that's not why you were confident. You were confident because you chose to be confident in response to telling off Mr. Buckner to his face. Although this might seem like a minor distinction, it's not. You control your confidence level. It's something you decide, not something that's bestowed on you by outside forces. You can choose to be confident at any time, regardless of the circumstances.

The Mood of the Humorist

Whether confident or not, if the humorist is passionate, upbeat, and having fun, their attempts at conversational humor will likely succeed.

If the humorist is hateful, passive-aggressive, bitter, frustrated, or self-indulgent, their attempts at conversational humor will likely fail.

If you're feeling pressure, or if you're feeling nervous about your attempts to be funny, you don't have to go through with it. You can try admitting you're nervous. A little radical honesty is a good way to get yourself in a more authentic, relaxed, and confident state.

A stubbornly positive and happy mood is not the ultimate goal when delivering humor. When a humorist is happy, the humor is best communicated when that happiness is masked periodically. When you "play it straight," concealing your true mood, you pretend not to realize what you're saying is intended to be funny. The way Leslie Nelson utters the classic line "And don't call me Shirley" in the movie *Airplane!* is a classic example of this practice in action.

When a humorist pretends they don't find their own humor amusing, the audience, whether it be one person, a few friends, or a stadium full of fans, is part of a sophisticated game of peekaboo in which the true mood of the teller is hidden for a moment. This facade of dry delivery is a character mask worn by the humorist that boosts the mood of the audience.

The Mood of the Audience

Humor will fail if an audience doesn't feel like laughing. The wise humorist assesses the state of every audience, regardless of its size, and strikes when the mood is right.

Being aware, as described in Chapter 3, is just the beginning. When you sharpen your focus to determine people's emotional states, you play a large part in determining when they're in the mood for humor. You can also influence their mood by setting the stage and taking into account all potential factors affecting an audience: what has come just before you and your humor, subtle or not-so-subtle social cues, and what's happening in the immediate environment that might affect or distract them, to name a few.

Just as we learn the important social skill of sensing the right time to communicate certain thoughts or feelings that aren't humorous, by tuning into the emotions of those around us, we learn the more advanced social skill of sensing the right time to communicate with humor.

Social Proof

When we hear other people laugh, we're more likely to laugh. TV sitcoms don't film in front of live studio audiences because production companies enjoy spending time and money managing large crowds and herding them into seats to magnanimously share the gift of laughter. They do it to sell a product, and the live studio audience is part of the pitch.

Producers of TV sitcoms aren't the only ones who can use this powerful humor lever. Surrounding yourself with people who enjoy your humor will encourage others to enjoy it. Directing your attention to the people giving your humor the best response is how you find your audience.

Some people won't like your humor. Not everybody likes everything. It doesn't make you a failure to have haters. We all have them. Focusing on those who like you, and being patient with those who don't, might ultimately turn the haters into likers.

Reputation

If you're known as a funny person, you have a leg up in the effort to create the right context for humor. You have a "brand voice" known for humor. Your reputation might precede you, and all the heavy lifting of convincing people to be in the mood for you and your style of humor will be done in advance. They'll understand and welcome your humorous communication. This is one of the many long-term fringe benefits of learning the skill of humor.

You can see this phenomenon in evidence with comedy movie stars and comedians. Wherever they go, people laugh with excitement sometimes before the celebrities even open their mouths. On *Inside Amy Schumer*, Amy joins a business call by saying "Hello," and the entire group of businesspeople cracks up laughing.

Context

Context is everything. Your confidence, your mood, the mood of your audience, and whether your humor is boosted by social proof or your reputation are components in the overall context of your humor.

Every other contextual element matters, too. What's the setting? What's the tension level? What's the vibe?

If you're performing at a comedy club, you're in a context where people understand that you'll try to be funny. If you write an essay in a humor magazine, audiences will understand your work within the context of the publication's history, layout, and design.

In person, out in the world, you have less control over such context, but the more you understand its effect, the more you can use it to your advantage.

On the subway, on the basketball court, and at home on a Sunday morning are all radically different contexts that will affect the way people perceive your humor. You have to assess each context carefully.

A classroom, library, or funeral might seem like the wrong time to be funny, but often these are the best places to introduce humor. People trapped in an environment where laughing is prohibited are primed to laugh. It can be a tinderbox where everyone inside is secretly waiting for the opportunistic humorist to strike a match.

Best Practices

- The character of the humorist is one of the most important ingredients in whether humor does its magic work of producing laughs.
- Confidence can make almost anything funny.
- Being aware of your own mood and the mood of your audience will dramatically improve the success of your humor.
- In humor, context is everything.

Exercises

1. Ask people you trust who won't sugarcoat the answer, "What kind of person am I?" Ask them to tell you how they would describe you in a few words to someone who didn't know you. Specifically, ask them how they would describe you when you're funny. Ask them to describe your sense of humor. Ask them what kind of character they think you are. Who would play you in a movie, and how would they accentuate your traits?
2. If you get some answers from Exercise 1 that you like and can accept, lean into this "branding" of yourself whenever you try to be funny.

CHAPTER

7

You Have the Floor

If you're one of those disgusting people who likes to spoon pure frosting into your mouth, please understand that most people prefer cake with their frosting.

The same goes for humor. Humor without a message is empty calories, and eventually, sensible people will get sick of it. Before we can frost a conversation with humor, we have to make the cake. The recipe for the cake is in this chapter. The recipe for the frosting is in Chapter 8 and beyond.

What is your message? What are you trying to say? What is your opinion about things? Your perspective on the world and what you think of it is the lens through which all your humor is delivered.

What you have to say may be a practical matter. Maybe you need to tell someone where you have to go or what you want to do, or you have a feeling you want to express. In all cases, you have information you feel is important, and you're compelled to communicate it.

Sometimes what you have to say is on the tip of your tongue. You don't need to make a stand-up routine or write an essay about it. You just need to communicate it to another person. It happens every time you talk:

"Mom, where's the whisk?"

"I'm having a bad week."

"Looks like a balloon to me."

"I like you."

Whatever you have to say, you can say it plainly, without frosting, or you can say it in a more delicious way, with humor:

"Mom, where's the whisk? I need it to save humanity."

"I'm having a such a bad week, my horoscope just said, 'Yikes.'"

"Looks like a deadly balloon attack to me."

"If you had a like button, I'd hit it."

In writing, your message is the point or theme of your article, essay, or script. It's what your characters have to say, or, more accurately, what you have to say through your characters.

How to Communicate

In almost all cases, you have a choice. You can communicate plainly or you can communicate humorously. If you struggle to express yourself with humor, consider the possibility that the problem might not be your dexterity with humor. You might be struggling to figure out what you have to say to begin with. If that's your struggle, this chapter will help you unlock whatever's in your brain that you're not telling us.

Your problem might be that you know what you have to say, but you struggle to say it in a funny way. If that's your problem, the subsequent chapters will help you.

In either case, let's start by getting clear on your message.

If you're a shy or quiet person, you might think you don't have anything to say. Maybe you prefer to be silent in most situations. If this is you, you probably have more to say than you realize. In fact, you probably have more to say than people who talk all the time. People who talk all the time lean heavily toward clown brain. They say a lot of what they're thinking without a filter. You, however, probably lean heavily toward editor brain. You filter what you have to say so much that sometimes nothing gets out.

We all have a bottomless well of things to say. Your brain fires off millions of synapses every millisecond. It's bursting with ideas. You have more things to say than you could possibly utter if you talked all day, every day, at 1,000 words a minute. There's a cauldron of interesting, funny, and outrageous opinions, comments, and thoughts bubbling in the recesses of your brain. You ignore most of them. Others rise to the surface and come out of your mouth like steam escaping from a covered pot.

Humor aside, it's healthy to let some of these thoughts out occasionally. If you don't, you live a life suppressed, with no outlet for this powerful, combustible brain fuel you produce every second.

You need these thoughts to create humor. They're your raw material, the coal you need to shovel into the furnace of your clown brain in order to power your funniness. Skilled humorists mine this deep store of ideas repeatedly and carefully, scooping some out every now and then when they need to summon a funny comment.

I HAVE
MANY OPINIONS

To vent this humor power, most of us turn to one (or both) of two outlets:

- A group of friends who allow us to say silly things we don't want to say around other people; these compatriots provide a safe space for us to be ourselves, let loose, and go prospecting in the depths of our minds.

- A journal where we spill out our unvarnished thoughts that aren't ready for public consumption.

How can we exploit this valuable resource and turn it into humor that can be confidently shared with everyone in our lives?

Internal Messages

Have you ever listened to a money guru talk about the best way to get rich? They claim that in order to earn more money, you first have to change the internal dialog you've had on a loop since childhood that formed your opinion about money and your sense of your own worth. They say phrases your parents used, like "We can't afford it" and "Money doesn't grow on trees," affect your ability to spend, save, and invest wisely.

Many of us are walking around repeating similar negative messages to ourselves about humor. We grow up being chided by parents, the school system, and the authorities of polite society: "Be quiet." "Behave." "That's not funny." "Stop being silly." "Act your age."

With these messages stamped into our impressionable heads for decades, most of us believe in our bones that what we have to say doesn't matter and isn't wanted, especially if it's something funny. We assume no one will take us seriously.

The result: we don't talk. We speak only when spoken to. We don't volunteer a comment, opinion, or thought. We certainly don't try to say anything funny. We keep it to ourselves.

Turning Thoughts into Humorous Thoughts

The first step toward using humor effectively is acknowledging that you have an unlimited power source of raw material inside you. If you're a person who doesn't say or do funny things very often, if you're self-identified (or identified by others) as an unfunny person, if you're not in the habit of producing funny writing, or if you're quiet, unassuming, or humorless, you might have rarely, if ever, tapped into your considerable warehouse of raw material, either consciously or unconsciously.

The second step, naturally, is to explore this inner gold mine. There are two excellent ways to begin, two practices that will open these strategic reserves. If you try these exercises, you might be surprised at the abundance of material you get to work with.

Free Writing

Free writing is an exercise that's been used by writers probably as long as writers have existed. Dorothea Brande wrote about it in her book, *Becoming a Writer*, in 1934. Julia Cameron popularized it in *The Artist's Way* a half-century later.

Free writing involves sitting down and writing without stopping, without knowing what to write, and without correcting or judging anything you write. You can do it on a notepad or computer. You can do it for any amount of time you want. Most people can do it for 20 minutes without any trouble. Set a timer for 10 minutes to start. Work your way up to 20, 30, or more.

What will you write during free writing? Whatever you want. Whatever comes to mind. It doesn't matter. Be honest. Lie. Pretend you're someone else. Have fun. You want as few guidelines and restraints as possible in this exercise. Avoid writing the same thing over and over. You don't want to be like Jack in *The Shining*. Try to express new thoughts continuously during this exercise. Keep the thoughts rolling. Expand on each one until you feel like changing the subject, and then change the subject. Be whimsical. Open the valve and let the ideas flow. Don't be embarrassed. No one will ever see this writing, unless you want to show it. It's for you alone, and you can delete it, crumple it up, or save it. You can write your opinions about any subject. You can write about how you feel. You can write about how frustrating it is to have to come up with things to write. You can tell stories. You can write things that amuse you.

If you do this exercise every day for a week, you might find that, after a few days, the floodgates will open. You might find you look forward to having this healing release of all your bottled-up thoughts. You might find yourself wanting to write for a longer period. You might find that you need it, and that the exercise is unblocking something deep inside you. You might find that it frees your mind.

On the flip side, you might find it difficult to come up with things to write about. You might find it difficult to do this exercise without judging what you write. You'll want to stop and go back and fix typos, or get the wording of a thought just right. Resist these impulses. Barrel forward like a fool. Just keep writing until your time is up.

Professional writers do this exercise for hours. There's a subset of self-published authors, led by Chris Fox, who count the number of words they write during these free writing sessions. They compete with themselves and others to write 5,000, 10,000, or more words per day. This way, they can write a first draft of a novel in as little as a week. Of course, this work needs a second and third draft, a lot of editing, and some feedback to truly take shape as a novel. But getting through a first draft is an important hurdle authors need to clear in order to make progress.

Free Talking

The second exercise is a variation on the first: free talking. Some people get more creative when they speak as opposed to when they write. If the free writing exercise feels like working against the grain for you, record yourself talking into the recorder app on your phone. If you live in the 1980s, record yourself on a cassette recorder. Hit "record" and start talking. Follow the guidelines of the free writing exercise. Talk about anything you want. Be honest. Be yourself. Or play a character. Talk in someone else's voice. Be silly.

One or both of these two simple exercises will reveal what you have to say, which is the foundation of humor. They're exercises that find out who you are and what you care about. They produce thoughts, opinions, and value judgments that can come only from you. They are the secret sauce of your humor.

The Opinion Generator

If the free writing and free talking exercises don't produce much beyond facts and figures not unique to you, there's a third exercise you can try: the opinion generator. It works like this: Write a series of random subjects (if you don't want to come up with your own subjects, or you're not sure what the subjects should be, just Google "list of random subjects") and then write your opinion about each subject. You'll find you have an opinion about everything. These should not be descriptions. They should not be adjectives. They should not be what other people think. They should be your opinions, ideally starting with *I* statements.

Examples:

- Subject: outer space

  Opinion: I like outer space. I'm fascinated by it. Fascinated by how vast it is. I can't even comprehend it, and that's amazing. I've always wanted to travel to outer space in a rocket.

- Subject: a recent election

  Opinion: I hate that it's always two entrenched party hacks who only represent the interests of the super-rich. Will I ever see a dynamic and effective leader who actually represents me and improves the lot of regular people in my lifetime?

- Subject: horses

  Opinion: I've never been a fan of horses. I don't understand why other people like them so much. They're big and actually kind of scary.

Make a list of 10 subjects and opinions like this. Remember, opinion only. *Big* is not an opinion about outer space. It's an adjective and a description. To truly tap your potential for humor, we need to know what makes you tick. We need to know what kind of person you are. The key to that is knowing what you're feeling and thinking.

Next, we'll turn all of these opinions into humor.

Best Practices

- Whatever you have to say can be said with humor.
- Humor requires a carrier message to be delivered to an audience.
- The source of all humor is the bottomless well of things you have to say that you're leaving unsaid.

Exercises

1. Try the free writing exercise for a few minutes every day. Set a timer and write with abandon. Try to increase the amount of time you spend on it as your interest and tolerance allows.
2. Try the free talking exercise for a few minutes every day. Say whatever's on your mind in your voice-note app. Try to increase the amount of time you spend on it as your interest and tolerance allows.
3. Try the opinion generator exercise. Write at least 10 sets of subjects and opinions.

With all three exercises, be honest, and don't worry about what other people might think of you. No one has to see or hear the results of these exercises.

8

The Funny Filters

You've mined the raw material you need to create humor: you have something to say. Now you need tools to mold your message into something funny. Humor, like many crafts, comes with its own set of specific tools needed to do the work. Sadly, you can't walk into a hardware store and buy these tools.

Comedy in the vaudeville days spawned a few physical "tools" that some people still associate with humor and comedy, props like the Groucho Marx nose glasses, the rubber chicken, baggy pants, the seltzer spray bottle, and the banana peel. In times gone by, a humorist who wielded one or more of these props was considered funny. They've been considered tacky for decades now.

Modern comics use physical tools as well. A subgroup among stand-up comedians is the prop comic, a performer who uses funny objects and makes jokes about them. Carrot Top is one of the most successful prop comics in recent years. Before him, Gallagher dabbled in props, most famously by smashing watermelons with a giant mallet. Julio Torres is the latest comedian to make it big with props.

Props bring a new dimension to these performers' comedy, and the tools are unique to each comedian. Unlike the vaudeville days, you and I can't use the same objects and expect the same hilarious results. In fact, we can expect the opposite. Once someone uses a comedy prop, it's considered unoriginal – even theft – for another comedian to use the same prop. The props, and any jokes associated with them, belong to the originator.

Performers aren't the only purveyors of humor to use tools. Writers of humor and comedy have tools as well: a computer with a word processing app, usually. Some use phones, notepads, or, if they live in the 1970s, typewriters.

Aside from these relics, props, and helpful appliances, there are no other physical tools of humor. There are tools, to be sure, but they only exist in our minds. The tools of humor are literary devices used to form humor out of our raw material generated in Chapter 7. There's a virtual humor workshop in our brains, and in it you'll find several tools hanging on a pegboard along the wall. There are 11, to be exact, and they are called the *funny filters*.

New Toys

The magic ingredient that creates humor in the written, spoken, and symbolic word is the funny filters. This is peekaboo for a sophisticated audience, representing a more advanced version of the part of the game where the performer's face is hidden. The funny filters do the hiding for us, but instead of hiding a face, they hide the true meaning of what we're saying.

These are the 11 funny filters:

- Irony
- Character
- Reference
- Shock
- Hyperbole
- Parody
- Wordplay
- Madcap
- Analogy
- Misplaced focus
- Metahumor

You'll have a chance to delve into each in the coming chapters.

In my book *How to Write Funny*, the guidebook for professional comedy writers, I lay out the 11 funny filters and how to use each to craft professional comedy. In this book, I'll introduce each and provide examples of its application for the layperson in conversational humor, humorous writing, and performance. No matter what level of interest you bring to the study of humor, you'll learn the basics of these tools and how to use them.

All 11 funny filters start with the same raw material: your message. The humor produced by one funny filter will be different than the humor produced by another. In this way, they're less like tools and more like wind instruments in an orchestra. Although they all take the same puff of human breath to make music, they each make a very distinct sound.

Another way to think of the funny filters is like toys. There's no right or wrong way to use them. There are best practices, which I'll list with each funny filter, but within these parameters, the humorist is encouraged to have fun, imagine, create, stack them like blocks, meld them like different colors of Play-Doh, and approach their use with a sense of curiosity, adventure, and play.

Yet another analogy that illustrates the nature of the funny filters is an imaginary meat grinder. Imagine putting the raw material (your message) in one end, and then turning the crank of your thoughts and watching delicious ground humor come out the other end.

The raw material, your message, is most likely not funny on its face. It's what scriptwriters call *on-the-nose* material, which is the scriptwriting term for dialog that conveys exactly what characters are thinking and/or feeling, as opposed to filtering it and concealing it like a wrapped gift or peekaboo game for the audience.

We can hide what we have to communicate behind all kinds of shields: symbolism, metaphor, passive-aggressiveness, anxiety, and more. Many of these games of concealment can be amusing. Some can be disturbing. The funny filters specifically conceal your message behind a shield that's funny.

Here are a few examples of on-the-nose versions of famous lines of dialog from movies. See how much more interesting and funny the lines are after they're filtered using the funny filters:

- On-the-nose version: "I will scare him so much that he accepts my offer." Filtered version: "I'll make him an offer he can't refuse."

  –Vito Corleone from *The Godfather* (Mario Puzo), using the character, analogy, misplaced focus, and shock funny filters.

- On-the-nose version: "I would like to experience sexual pleasure, also." Filtered version: "I'll have what she's having."

  –Diner in *When Harry Met Sally* (Rob Reiner and Nora Ephron), using the misplaced focus and shock funny filters.

- On-the-nose version: "That is correct." Filtered version: "That's a bingo!"

  –Hans Landa, *Inglourious Basterds* (Quentin Tarantino) using the irony, character, shock, madcap, and wordplay funny filters.

You can turn your plain, on-the-nose thoughts into humor using the same funny filters. If you want to eat at Arthur Treacher's Fish & Chips, for example, you could communicate your message on-the-nose: "I want to eat at

Arthur Treacher's Fish & Chips." Or you could run your message through some funny filters first, communicating the same idea but with a humorous tone:

- "Let's eat at Arthur Treacher's Fish & Chips before it's plundered by pirates." (the shock and hyperbole funny filter)
- "Tonight, the romantic scoundrel Arthur Treacher will take me as his concubine." (the character and misplaced focus funny filters)
- "Let's eat out at Fartin' Bleeper's Piss and Chimps." (the wordplay, shock, and parody funny filters)
- [In an old-time TV announcer voice] "Honey, I think the whole family would enjoy Arthur Treacher's Fish & Chips tonight. It's Fish-licious!" (the character, parody, and wordplay funny filters)
- [crawling on the ground like someone starving in the desert] ". . . need Arthur . . . Treacher's . . . Fish . . . & Chips." (the madcap and character funny filters)

Without the funny filters, messages are delivered blandly. You can go through life being a bland, non-humorous communicator by habitually communicating on-the-nose, like an AI-generated voice, or you can opt to color what you say with humor using the funny filters.

The funny filters work together or separately. Each one can be turned up and heightened to a different degree. And because there are 11, some with their own subsets, they offer billions of possible combinations and variations.

Using the funny filters is like tuning an equalizer on a home stereo. The same audio signal might be coming through, but if you turn up the bass or turn down the treble, the sound comes out different. The funny filters create an equalizer for your thoughts with 11 different settings. You can use some funny filters and not others, turn each one all the way up or all the way down, or leave it neutral.

A final analogy: the funny filters are like spices. You can have more of some than others. You can focus only on one. By combining different funny filters, you create a different flavor of humor. Have fun mixing, matching, and experimenting.

Here's how they work in interpersonal situations: when you have an opinion, thought, instruction, or comment – anything you want to say – before you say it, scroll through the rolodex of the funny filters in your mind to determine if you can say it through the prism of one or more of the funny filters. When you pick one, say it.

The process is similar to the way the Terminator's electronic brain gave him a multiple-choice list of options for what to say to the hotel janitor who knocked on the door and asked, "Do you have a dead cat in there, or what?" The Terminator's readout said:

Possible answers:

- Yes/no.
- Go away.
- Please come back later.
- Fuck you, asshole.
- Fuck you.

Much as you will attempt to do with the funny filters, the Terminator selected the funniest answer: "Fuck you, asshole." (the shock, irony, reference, wordplay, misplaced focus, and character funny filters).

The Funny Filters in Conversation

The speed required to come up with funny things to say in person puts tremendous pressure on the humorist. Some people thrive in this pressure-cooker environment. The extra surge of adrenalin they get from being on the spot helps them select a good comment. Others crumble under the pressure and decide not to say anything.

Deciding not to say anything is okay. If you don't do well under pressure, bow out. Get used to the funny filters in low-pressure situations for now, like with your close friends who don't care if you fail and say something stupid, or with strangers who will never see you again.

To get more proficient with humor, you'll have to practice this process. Go at your own pace, and make sure you're only proceeding if you enjoy it. The more you try, the better you'll get. And the better you get, the more you'll enjoy it and the quicker your wit will get. It's the quick wits who can run their message through all the funny filters, create a Terminator-like list of options, and select a good one without delay.

Start with one funny filter at a time. Though you'll find it's almost impossible not to pair them or triple them, a frequent mistake aspiring humorists make is doing too much and complicating their humor. Simple is always better. Learn the ground rules before you fly.

The funny filters are laid out in the following 11 chapters in no particular order, although the more traditionally easy to use are listed first. If you decide to go through this book sequentially and do the exercises, this ordering should help you catch on nicely.

Humor is a game of averages. Not all humor gets laughs. These 11 funny filters, used properly, will give your humor the best chance to succeed. There's no hope for humor that doesn't employ at least one of the funny filters. They are as essential to the creation of humor as the periodic table of elements is to the creation of chemicals.

The funny filters work the same way in written humor as in conversational humor. The only difference is that in a piece of prose, script, or written comedy routine, you can take as much time as you need to think it through.

Humor Preferences

Some people like some funny filters more than others. Our individual funny filter preference is what gives us our unique sense of humor. Some people don't like shock humor. Some don't like madcap. However, the more funny filters you use, the more you'll connect with a variety of people. Professional comedians and humorists try to use all 11 funny filters as often as they can. For interpersonal communication, it's wise to get a sense of which funny filters will connect best with each person you talk to.

Some people prefer subtle humor; others prefer goofy, hit-you-over-the-head humor. This variety can be achieved using each funny filter. They can all be used in a basic way to create a subtle or wry effect. They can also be used in a heightened way to create a broad effect. Heightening funny filters is like using a volume dial. It can push the tool to its extreme, exaggerating it, giving it an assist from one or more additional funny filters, backing up words with actions, raising the stakes, or adding more specificity. Examples of how to heighten will come in each funny filter's chapter.

Best Practices

- Use the funny filters to convert plain, informational messages into humor.
- To create humor that has a chance of succeeding, you must use one or more of the 11 funny filters.
- Use the funny filters like toys. Experiment, and have fun.

Exercises

1. Express a statement, opinion, or value judgment about a random subject. Use the following subjects or make up your own.
2. Riff on your opinion and try to be funny. Incorporate some of the mindset tips from the preceding chapters: have fun, relax, be yourself, and let go of any pressure to be funny. You might find you already have an instinctual understanding of the funny filters.

Examples:

- Subject: outer space

  Opinion: Outer space seems exciting because of all the space movies and the potential for alien life, but I hate outer space. I want nothing to do with it. It would take you a million years just to reach one of these aliens and say hello, so what's the point?

- Subject: a recent election

  Opinion: This is the best we can do? These phonies in suits? Maybe instead of voting we could pit them against each other in a fight to the death. I might finally take an interest in politics.

- Subject: horses

  Opinion: Horses are supposed to be romantic and beautiful and all that, but they stink, and they're dumb. Dogs are a hundred times smarter. They're just as disgusting but at least they've figured out how to live indoors. Horses are losers.

9

Isn't It Ironic

Our first funny filter is irony. Irony is one of the simplest funny filters to use, and one of the most common. It deals in a basic concept most of us learn as kids: opposites. At the same time, it's also one of the most powerful funny filters. It can bring enormous scale to a humorous concept.

When your literal meaning is the opposite of your intended meaning, you have irony. But irony can be used in myriad other ways to create humor in conversation, drama, images, and more.

How Irony Works

Irony is in play when the stark contrast between opposites is highlighted. An easy way to start with irony is to identify your message and then send it through the irony funny filter, which produces the opposite of your message.

With irony, you don't so much run it through a complicated filtering machine as imagined in the previous chapter. All you do is reflect it in a mirror. You take what you have to say and flip it around.

"I'm tired – it's time for bed" becomes "I'm not tired." Heightened, it becomes "I feel like running a marathon!"

"I need to study everything there is to know about earthworms for this important essay I'm writing" becomes "I don't need to learn anything about earthworms." Heightened, it becomes "It's very important that I never learn another fact about earthworms as long as I live."

You can use irony with any statement. You get the best fodder when the statement is an opinion or value judgment.

Sarcasm is a type of irony. When a parent serves broccoli to a sullen teen, and the teen says, "Oh, thank you, I *love* broccoli" with an eye roll and a mocking tone, the teen is using sarcasm. One of the simplest ways to use irony, sarcasm is also one of the least effective. It's more annoying than funny. It produces a weaker effect in two ways. First, using the example of the teen, the contrast between opposites isn't convincing because we know the teen isn't telling the truth. Second, the "just kidding" moment comes too soon. The tone gives it away. Humor requires a moment when the audience takes the humorist seriously at first. The teen could use pure irony by saying the same thing in a convincing tone while surreptitiously passing the broccoli to the dog. The contrast between opposites (expressing a sincere love for broccoli while feeding it to the dog) is sharp and specific. This comment would be funnier to other siblings at the table, and possibly even to the parents.

Irony works especially well when it's heightened, when the opposites are stretched to the extreme.

Simple Comparisons

Sometimes funny filters can suggest ideas for humorous comments by themselves, without the need of raw material (a message). Simply pointing out irony as you observe it in the world, comparing two things that are polar opposites, can be amusing. Every day we see wildly contrasting things: two objects, two personalities, two situations – anything. Some examples:

- Something big compared to something small
- Something important compared to something trivial
- Something needed compared to something unnecessary
- Something smart compared to something dumb
- Something new compared to something old

To turn these comparisons into humor, simply comment on the difference, or ask yourself the question that can spur a humorous thought, "If this is true, what else is true?"

THE NEW CORPORATE HEADQUARTERS IN IRONY FALLS, IOWA

A lot of people have difficulty with the concept of opposites. It's a strange, ephemeral way of looking at things, and it only comes with a handful of obvious examples most people can agree on: hard and soft, hot and cold, big and small. How do you determine the opposite of, say, grass? A car? A chicken? What's the opposite of history? There are no obvious answers. We can all chose our own. The humorist has the power to frame opposites as needed to achieve the goal of making people laugh. An audience need not agree. Some possible answers: the opposite of grass could be concrete. The opposite of a car could be a truck, or it could be walking. The opposite of a chicken could be a duck. Or it could be an egg. The opposite of history is probably the future.

If you ever watched *Sesame Street*, you might remember the show's excellent series of primers on opposites, which demonstrated how to think about irony, such as in cartoons like "You Can Find the Opposite."

If you struggle with the concept of opposites, try defining some opposites as you go through your day. Compare your answers with others.

Dramatic Irony

Another way to use irony in humor is with dramatic irony. Storytellers use dramatic irony to supply the audience with more information than the characters, which creates suspense. Alfred Hitchcock provided the example of characters sitting around a table having a conversation. The scene is boring. But when the same characters are sitting around the same table having a conversation while, unknown to them, a bomb is ticking under the table, the scene is suspenseful.

In humor, dramatic irony can come through attitude. In peekaboo, the humorist pretends to be unaware of what's happening and expresses surprise when the face reappears, imitating the audience's presumed experience. In more complex humor, dramatic irony is displayed as a lack of awareness in the hilarity of the material.

This lack of awareness isn't required for humor, but it can amplify its effect. Cluelessness can be expressed as a light suggestion of "who me?" It can also be expressed through a "straight" performance, where a strict adherence to a character, voice, or action belies any knowledge that humor is taking place. The way Stephen Colbert played his character on *The Colbert Report* is an excellent example of a straight performance.

"Playing it straight" is also called *dry*, as described in Chapter 6. Dry humor is stripped of its emotion so the audience can't tell what the humorist's true feelings might be. If irony were a dial from 1 to 10, sarcasm would be a 1 and dry humor would be a 10.

Practice irony by saying the opposite of what you mean. Do it in an obvious way, with sarcasm, and do it in a dry way, playing it straight, and see how it feels. See how it fits with your personality. See what kind of reaction you get.

Of course, there are many ways to use irony in between sarcasm and playing things straight. You can play with it any way you want and discover what works best for you.

Irony Examples

Joseph Heller uses irony repeatedly in *Catch-22*:

- Airmen who are considered insane can be relieved from combat duty, but anyone who requests to be grounded due to insanity is considered sane enough to fly.
- A character sells contraband to the enemy, yet he's celebrated as a hero for his entrepreneurial spirit.
- A character is described as so likable that no one can stand him.

Another example of irony in the written word is *The Onion*, which purports to be a serious news organization, yet the silly content of its stories demonstrates the opposite.

Terry Gilliam's iconic cartoons in *Monty Python's Flying Circus* provide a broader illustration of the use of irony. Big objects clash with small objects. Crude, low-brow images clash with classy, high-brow images. It's a parade of opposites. Much of this irony happens in the background while other types of humor, including structured animated sketches, exist in the foreground, creating a kind of subterranean layer of irony that elevates the entire cartoon, making it consistently amusing.

Del Close, the godfather of the Second City Theater and Training Center, is counted as a mentor to three generations of the most popular comedy stars in the world: Bill Murray, Tina Fey, John Belushi, Mike Myers, Amy Poehler, and many others. His scant career as a film actor is remembered today for one role, a bit part in *Ferris Bueller's Day Off.* In a spectacular illustration of irony, he plays the world's most boring teacher, when in fact his teaching has probably brought more entertainment to the world than any single individual. His scene is further heightened by using the additional funny filters of character, reference, madcap, misplaced focus, wordplay, and metahumor.

An example of irony in conversation: "I had the idea of a lifetime today. It could transform the world and make me a billion dollars. Then I walked into another room and couldn't remember it."

Using Irony

How do you turn irony into humor if you're not legendary visual artist Terry Gilliam, mentor-to-the-stars Del Close, or brilliant filmmaker John Hughes (writer-director of *Ferris Bueller*)?

The answer is, any way you want. The funny filters are a playground, and irony is one of the jungle gyms. Start by identifying or creating two things that are polar opposites, and then talk or write about them. The way you use irony can accentuate both your unique sense of humor and the meaning of what you're saying. You can observe irony and point it out, coloring it with your perspective. You can put yourself in the equation and find your opposite. You can dryly pretend to have the opposite of your opinion. You can use sarcasm or play it straight. You can also combine irony with other funny filters, as you'll see in the chapters ahead.

Best Practices

- Use irony by comparing and contrasting polar opposites.
- Try anything from sarcasm to dry humor to explore irony's range.

Exercises

1. Notice things that are opposites.
2. Say, write, or do something ironic by playing with the idea of the opposites you've discovered.
3. Experiment with different levels of irony, from sarcasm to playing it straight, to see what works best for you.

CHAPTER

10

What a Character

Do you know someone who's funny but doesn't realize they're funny? How about someone you'd describe as having "a personality"? These are characters. We love characters, real or imagined. We're fascinated by them, and we find them funny. When they behave in particular ways that define them, we delight in their predictability.

In real life, characters make us laugh without trying. They entertain just by being themselves. In humor, the character funny filter is just about everyone's favorite toy in the toy chest. The humorist can harness the raw energy of other people and sharpen it, channeling personalities into humor.

How Character Works

You can become a characterization of yourself, taking on the role of a simple character by acting and/or speaking like someone else. You can also write in the voice of a character in prose or script format. You can draw a character. You can allude to a character or vaguely suggest one. In all instances, the voice of the character becomes the vessel through which your message becomes funny, coloring it with personality and familiar traits that amuse your audience.

When a humorist introduces a character with a trait or traits discernible to an audience, the seed of humor is planted. When a character takes action, and that action is motivated by the character's established trait or traits, humor blossoms.

The traits that can define a humorous character are endless. For the best chance at humor, the traits should indicate a weakness or frailty, especially one we identify in ourselves to a lesser degree. They can be general traits:

- Lovable
- Childlike
- Naive
- Impish
- Sad
- Anxious
- Angry
- Devious

Or they can be specific traits:

- Always has a personal emergency
- Perpetually unprepared or running late
- Gripped by an irrational fear
- Burns everything they cook
- Is a terrible but enthusiastic singer
- Can't resist throwing things away
- Can't resist hoarding everything

The moment an audience witnesses a character acting in accordance with an identified trait is usually the precise moment they laugh. As with all the funny filters, heightening makes these moments funnier. To heighten a character, sharpen it to one or two obvious traits, and then demonstrate the character acting in accordance with those traits in extreme circumstances, when the stakes are high, or when other funny filters are also being used.

Characters in Context

Characters in a story are the key to its effectiveness. Audiences pay attention and get carried away by a narrative when they empathize with its characters, whether dramatic or comedic. Characters teach us how to behave in the world by showing us a counter example. Their outrageous behavior makes us feel good about our own sensible behavior. In drama, this good feeling teaches us a lesson or gives us an opportunity to reflect on the myriad choices in life. In comedy, this good feeling makes us laugh.

When a character wants something in an obsessive way, that single-minded drive can be funny, especially if the desire motivates extreme actions, is combined with other funny filters, or is heightened in other ways.

Dramatic characters are more complex than humorous characters. Real-life characters are the most complex of all – contradictory, too. They can have a million traits. In humor, characters are simple and two-dimensional. They're reduced to a few key traits or archetypes. This makes them quantifiable and understandable to audiences. Humorous characters are like cardboard standees that represent real humans, but with only a handful of traits. Anything more would be too confusing for the brief time they're needed to make something funny.

Dramatic and real-life characters can instantly become humorous if they "drop" momentarily into a more simplified characterization featuring just a few traits or a single trait.

Character Examples

So many wonderful and entertaining characters have delighted audiences since the dawn of entertainment. Each one is an example of the character funny filter.

Charlie Brown is a sad sack who always gets the worst hand dealt to him. When he runs to kick the football, we know how it will turn out. What's surprising is the different lies Lucy tells him and the different reasons he has to be optimistic. Still, he'll never kick that football. This is the character funny filter in action: a well-defined character acting in accordance with well-established traits.

Ron Burgundy is a bumbling authority. In *Anchorman: The Legend of Ron Burgundy*, Will Ferrell and Adam McKay establish one of the character's central traits early in the movie: he will read anything in the teleprompter. Later, his nemesis Veronica Corningstone changes his famous sign-off at the end of the news broadcast from "Stay classy, San Diego" to "Go fuck yourself, San Diego." When he reads it live on air, it produces one of the biggest laughs in the movie. This is the character funny filter in action again: a well-defined character acting in accordance with well-established traits.

Del Close's character in *Ferris Bueller's Day Off* has one trait: he's boring. As a minor character in only one scene, this is all he needs.

In prose, Ignatius J. Reilly, from John Kennedy Toole's classic novel, *A Confederacy of Dunces*, is lazy, overeducated, and hates humanity. Tom Sawyer is another well-known prose character. His traits: he's a trickster with a good heart.

In real-life, imagine Aunt Beatrice is a camping enthusiast who loves Sno Balls, those pink chocolate cakes with the creamy center. She's a character with two traits. If you catch her sneaking out of the tent in the middle of the night to devour an entire box of Sno Balls, and then fighting with a ravenous raccoon for control of the box, you might laugh. Why would this scene be funny to you? Because you know the character: Aunt Beatrice. You know the character's traits: she likes Sno Balls and camping. You see her acting in accordance with these traits in an extreme way, and voila, laughs result.

Aunt Beatrice is an example of a person with deep complexity and contradictions, a fully dimensional personality. However, by dropping her into two identifiable traits (enjoying camping and loving Sno Balls), she's diminished in a humorous way.

Character Archetypes

In my book *How to Write Funny Characters*, I spell out the 40 most popular archetypes in comedy with specific guidelines on how to use each most effectively. Here are a few of the most commonly used character archetypes:

- **The everyperson:** a normal and relatable character who observes the zaniness of other characters. The everyperson serves as a reflection of the audience – like a friend or confidant. Dave Barry steps into this role in his columns and books. TV sitcoms often have an everyperson character at the center who's surrounded by kooks. Kristen Wiig's character in *Bridesmaids* was an everyperson. The everyperson archetype is also popular in stand-up. Dave Chappelle, Kathleen Madigan, and Jerry Seinfeld are examples. To assay this role in your life, or to drop into this character, make yourself relatable by using the reference funny filter. (See Chapter 11.)

- **The grown-up child:** anyone who acts like a child, displaying more emotion than situations warrant. We enjoy this character because it shows us how far we've come in controlling our emotions as adults. It gets an extra boost of humor from its inherent irony (a full-grown person acting like a toddler is opposites at play). Elmer Gantry, from Sinclair Lewis's novel of the same name, and Pip, from Charles Dickens' *Great Expectations*, are examples of the grown-up child. Although not a particularly popular archetype in stand-up comedy (Kevin Hart being a notable exception), it's an extremely popular archetype in TV, movies, and cartoons. Will Farrell often plays the grown-up child, most clearly in *Elf* and *Step Brothers*. In real life, if you pretend to sob when TCBY is out of your favorite frozen-yogurt flavor, you momentarily drop into this archetype.

- **The trickster:** a lovable scamp who holds out bananas and then yanks them away. Dr. Seuss's Cat in the Hat is a famous trickster on the printed page. Johnny Depp's Captain Jack Sparrow in the *Pirates of the Caribbean* movies is a trickster. Stand-up comics who lead on audiences or subvert their expectations are tricksters.

They do this with the misplaced focus funny filter. (See Chapter 18.) Anthony Jeselnek is a prime example. Any comedian can temporarily drop into the trickster archetype when outsmarting a heckler. In real life, the trickster is a practical joker, bringing delight to the people in their lives with unexpected gags, misdirects, or hoaxes.

- **The crank:** a grumpy character who complains about everything. Notable cranks include Oscar the Grouch from *Sesame Street*, stand-up comics Lewis Black, George Carlin, and Roseanne Barr, and Carl Fredricksen in the movie *Up*. Two of the most famous cranks in literature are Charles Dickens's Ebenezer Scrooge and Dr. Seuss's Grinch. To play or drop into the crank archetype in real-life conversation, you just need a reason to hate something and then express it like you're an old man on his porch, yelling at kids.

Is Everyone a Character?

Everyone is a character sometimes. We're all complicated individuals, but sometimes we drop into an archetype in a funny moment, or we slip into archetypal behavior more habitually. You might know a real-life crank, for example (or maybe you are one). Different people are funny for different reasons. They suggest different archetypes. The character funny filter is a reduction – a grand simplification – of the nuances and variety that make us amusing to other people, and other people to us.

The character funny filter can be applied to any kind of living or personified individual: an animal, an alien, a spirit being, or an organization. Popular cat and dog videos go viral because they employ the character funny filter. We see ourselves in them, we empathize with them, and we recognize the animals' traits with great affection. Even an inanimate object can be a funny character. If a humorist decides to imbue a stapler with a personality, it can be funny using the same principles.

Characters work best when they're empathetic, especially if they're protagonists in a story. This is done by making them complex and relatable, with positive and negative traits. A minor character in a smaller role, or a character reference in a single joke, doesn't need to be complex or even empathetic. They can be one-note. A humorous character only needs to be complex enough to fill the amount of time they occupy in a story.

Successful stand-up comedians always have an identifiable persona, an established archetype that highlights their flaws. They pretend to lack awareness of these flaws, which invites audiences to laugh at them. Maria Bamford is a kook. Bill Burr is a psycho. Leslie Jones is a fighter.

Where Is the Surprise in Character?

If we laugh at characters by delighting in their predictability, where is the surprise that all humor requires? Where is the reveal of the face in the peekaboo game or the pulling away of the banana at the last minute? With character, the surprise comes from being predictably unpredictable. We know what characters' traits are. What surprises us is how they act them out. What zany antics will ensue when these characters reveal their traits in new situations?

If a kook archetype walks down the street, we might know they're a kook, but we don't know what they'll do that's kooky. If the kook spots a realtor's ad on the side of a bus bench that says, "Hello, I'm Becky," the kook might nod at first, and then say, "Hello Becky, my name is Chris. You are beautiful. May I buy your house?" Or the kook might offer to improve Becky's makeup with a tube of roll-on deodorant fashioned into lipstick. The reveal is what we crave.

Steve Carell's kook character from *The Legend of Ron Burgundy* satisfied this craving to make one of the funniest supporting characters and kook archetypes in movie history.

Another way to achieve surprise using the character funny filter is by combining it with other funny filters. For example, you can combine irony with character to create character irony. This is when characters behave in the opposite way that we expect, given their well-established traits. The *Simpsons* episode where Homer becomes a super genius uses character irony.

In a famous *SNL* sketch, the character of Ronald Reagan (played by Phil Hartman) repeatedly drops into character irony. Hartman portrays Reagan as a doddering fool who rolls out his slow "Aw, shucks" persona for a photo op with a Girl Scout, but after the photographer and Girl Scout leave, Reagan transforms into a sharp, fast-talking, and decisive leader who speaks fluent Arabic and can handle several high-stakes crises at the same time.

Best Practices

- Use the character funny filter by identifying one to three simple traits in a character and then showing the character acting on those traits.
- Use character archetypes for best results.
- Drop any character from fiction or real life into a simple characterization to create humor.

Exercises

1. List some of your favorite funny characters. What makes them funny to you? How would you define their traits? Are they an identifiable archetype?
2. List a few simple traits that could serve to identify you if you had to describe yourself in a sentence or two.
3. Create a funny character and put the character in a story.

11

A Point of Reference

Do you struggle to relate to people in conversation? Maybe when you first meet someone, you feel a slight panic, leaving you grasping for something to say.

What most of us do in these situations is try to think of something we have in common. When you do this, you might feel like a comedian starting a bit: "Did you ever notice how . . .?" or "Don't you hate it when . . .?" or "Did you hear about . . .?"

When comedians do this, they're setting up a joke based on the reference funny filter, a tool of humor we can all use, not just to make humor but also to connect with people.

How Reference Works

Reference is a tool of humor people use in any kind of exchange that involves a shared experience. It's a pleasant bonding moment that often makes us laugh.

Jerry Seinfeld is famous for this type of humor. In stand-up, use of the reference funny filter is called *observational comedy*. Comedians who use it point out something they've observed – about being a human being, living in society, or anything – that they believe audiences will recognize. This simple recognition, depending on how astute the observation is, can result in a spark of humor.

The challenge with reference is choosing just the right level of awareness in the audience. An obvious reference like "Did you ever notice how you get really tired at night?" is too obvious to generate laughs or build a connection. On the flip side, a reference that's too obscure, like "Did you ever notice how the apigenin can increase the function of the chloride channel and cause hyperpolarization?" won't connect with anyone. (However, it might still get laughs with the madcap [Chapter 16] and metahumor [Chapter 19] funny filters.)

Selecting a reference that's in the sweet spot between these two extremes has a good chance of producing a humorous result. The chances improve further if the reference involves a frailty we all share, something that's slightly off about the culture, society, or human condition. A reference is best if it's something the audience has noticed in their own lives but never thought about consciously.

Finding an astute, original observation is the trickiest part of the reference funny filter. It requires practice and, in some cases, a testing process. Comedians gauge the level of awareness in audiences constantly, performing in different venues to try different references with different crowds. You may not want or even have the ability to test everything you say or write to make sure it connects with people. You can still learn plenty by thinking of every casual exchange as a test. What are conversations if not tests to see how much of a shared experience you and the person you're talking with can establish?

If you think about communication in this way, it can become easier to test, both verbally and in writing. It can be fun. You can ask someone if they can relate to a scenario you're experiencing. When you find the sweet spot, you'll get a nod, a smile, and perhaps a laugh.

If you're a natural conversationalist, you've surely used the reference funny filter many times. You've also gained a good sense of topics or observations that are reliable and appropriate. You naturally engage in banter that you believe the person or people you're talking to will find interesting and not too obvious or obscure.

If you don't consider yourself a natural conversationalist, or if you tend to clam up in social situations, the idea of the reference funny filter may be new to you. You'll need to experiment to learn where the sweet spot is. Impromptu conversation can feel like an anxiety-inducing cage match for many of us, and it's the most challenging way to use reference. Trying to create grade-A material off the top of your head is challenging for anyone. You have to think fast. You can work up to it by trying to write instead, using journaling, emails, or humorous essays to find reference topics and ideas you can bring up later in conversation.

How to Find Reference

To find more astute points of reference that have the best chance of creating humor, start with prompts like these and simply finish the sentences:

- "Have you heard of . . .?"
- "Did you read about . . .?"
- "Have you seen . . .?"
- "Have you noticed when . . .?"

You can talk about an experience that happened to you, a social interaction, or a little struggle you're having in your life. Observations that are universal, relatable, and that engender a touch of sympathy are especially fruitful. Lighter, noncontroversial subject matter works best for the amateur humorist. Anything potentially traumatizing, disturbing, or dark can suck the humor potential out of your words like an industrial vacuum. Leave such topics to the stand-up comedians and professional humor writers. They're the experts at making controversial subjects funny.

Observations on the lighter side of life are fertile ground for conversational humor. These are the kinds of references used by "clean comedians" like Chonda Pierce and Jim Gaffigan. You may have watched and enjoyed their comedy or comedy like theirs as a passive listener. Watch them now with an ear toward identifying the points of reference they use. What have they observed and how are they sharing it? Listen to how the audience recognizes the references and laughs on cue.

Reference Examples

Here are some random observations on the lighter side of life:

- The walk button on stop lights is a hoax. Pressing it isn't going to make the light change faster.
- Who thought men and women should live together? They're incompatible. Gyms and locker rooms have the right idea – keep them separate.
- Why do we say, "Sorry, I missed your call"? Is anyone so hurt by a missed call that they need an apology?

- We need to stop reading online reviews. The people writing those aren't trusted consumer-product experts. They're just regular idiots.

- Why do people have to fill every quiet moment with small talk? Shut up! I'm enjoying some peace.

Avoiding Clichés

A common pitfall in all humor is the use of clichés. (Remember Chapter 1: Don't use canned jokes.) Clichés are phrases, jokes, or humorous topics that are well-worn enough that just about everyone has heard them at least once before. A cliché in the context of reference is an observation that is not only too obvious but also in common use.

The rule for clichés is simple: if you've heard a joke or funny phrase before, don't repeat it as your own. It's only acceptable to repeat it with credit from the source, if you have it. The rules are more lenient with clichéd subject matter. It's only stealing if you steal someone's exact wording. No one owns subject matter. However, in the mind of the audience, a clichéd subject will result in a groan or at least a subconscious feeling that your humor is not very good.

The problem with clichés for the nonprofessional humorist is that new ones are introduced every day. Unless your full-time job is staying on top of evolving trends in language, how can you expect to keep up? The hundreds of amateur and professional comedians and humorists in the How to Write Funny Facebook group have you covered.

Our complete list of modern clichés to avoid is updated frequently at howtowritefunny.com/list.

Using Reference with an Existing Message

Reference is typically a starting point, but it can sometimes inspire a message and give you an idea for something to say:

- Isn't it the worst when you accidentally throw something away and you have to go digging in the trash for it?
- Why do people always ask, "How was your flight?"
- Squirrels hate me.

You can also use the reference funny filter to make an existing message more humorous. Start with your message, which let's say is "We should sell our couch." Then, try to think of any aspect of that message that could be relatable to others. What is an unusual, unique, or fun detail about your message that others have probably experienced?

- Finding coins in the cushions
- Stains
- Being seated

Then, incorporate one of these into your message to make it more humorous:

- Let's sell our couch, but first let's dig out every coin to maximize profit.

- We should list our couch for sale. I'll Photoshop the stains out.
- If we sell the couch, I'll be left with many fond memories of being seated.

Reference is an excellent building block that other funny filters fit nicely on top of. You can demonstrate reference through a character. You can hyperbolize it (coming up in Chapter 14). You can start with a reference and then make it ironic: "How was my flight? It was amazing, like riding a rainbow!"

You'll find new ways to double- and triple-up the funny filters in the pages ahead to increase your humor batting average.

Other Types of Reference Humor

In-jokes, where only a small subset of people understand the context, are another form of the reference funny filter. In-jokes are particularly bonding in one-on-one conversations.

References don't always have to be astute observations about modern life. They can refer to the weather, a new movie, or sports scores. These kinds of references are not usually funny by themselves. They need augmentation by other funny filters or more specific details.

A callback joke, a subset of the in-joke, is another powerful form of reference that's easy to use. Simply refer to a funny observation again after having left it alone for a while. This almost always gets a laugh. In a comedy script, a *runner* is a joke that's called back more than once.

Best Practices

- Notice anything you think others might also have noticed that they might not have thought of consciously.
- Find the sweet spot of reference by observing things that aren't too obscure or too common.

Exercises

1. Start a written list of observations or experiences that you think other people have observed or experienced. Write them down as you notice them.
2. Point out some of your observations in conversation and see if people can relate to your experience.
3. Write a short paragraph that expounds on one of your observations to express your opinion about it.

12

Shock and Outrage

In Chapter 8, I promised to lay out the funny filters starting with the easiest to use. Shock is probably the easiest, but I didn't want to start with it. That would be like showing a houseguest your sex dungeon first.

Shock is so easy to use, in fact, professional comedy writers and humorists often refer to certain shock-based jokes as "too easy."

Shock is a funny filter you've heard about before, regardless of your experience with humor. Jokes that succeed purely from shock value are jokes that use the shock funny filter.

If you enjoy shock humor, this funny filter will be a treat for you. If you find shock humor distasteful, the information in this chapter might help you understand and appreciate its appeal. Like all the funny filters, shock can be used to create humor that anyone can love. It can even be used to create clean comedy.

Shock humor, or humor that uses the shock funny filter, is one of the more extreme ways to replicate the "boo" aspect of the peekaboo nature of humor. The emphasis in shock is almost always on the surprise.

The idea of "appropriate" humor usually means humor that doesn't employ too much of the shock funny filter. But isn't a little bit of inappropriateness what most of us are looking for in our humor? We want to feel like we're laughing at something we shouldn't laugh at, like we're getting away with something. This sense of guilty pleasure is what makes the shock funny filter so fun.

How Shock Works

Any light-hearted mention of something you wouldn't deem appropriate to mention around children or mixed company has the potential to create humor. Inserting a reference to sex, drugs, bodily functions, violence (along with a host of subcategories) in an otherwise clean sentence is all it takes to create humor with the shock funny filter. Swearing is also a prime feature of shock.

Whether you're just starting out, trying to incorporate humor in conversation or writing, or you're a professional humorist, the best practice with shock is to use it sparingly. Topics like death, cartoonish violence, or things that are gross, somewhat controversial, sacred to some, scary to others – or even just religion and politics – can make for shock humor that most audiences will accept if used in moderation.

To demonstrate how a touch of shock can create humor in an otherwise humorless statement, here are some examples:

- Dry, humorless statement: "I'm cold."
  Same statement with a dash of the shock funny filter: "I'm freezing my tits off."

- Dry, humorless statement: "I like this soup."
  Same statement with a dash of the shock funny filter: "This soup is fucking delicious."

- Dry, humorless statement: "It's a spider!"
  Same statement with a dash of the shock funny filter: "It's a spider! Kill it! For the love of God, kill it!"

- Dry, humorless statement: "I voted for this guy, and I don't like him."
  Same statement with a dash of the shock funny filter: "I'll see you in the camps."

- Dry humorless statement: "I need to use the bathroom. Where is it?"

  Same statement with a dash of the shock funny filter: "Where the crapper at?"

Any of these statements could be heightened by adding irony, character, or other funny filters. For example, you could introduce the character archetype of the royal, which is any kind of rich, uppity character, to heighten the use of shock by creating an opposing force. When spoken in an English accent, the result combines shock, character, and irony: "Dear Madam, would you kindly direct me to the crapper?"

The Appetite for Shock

Both tone and awareness of an audience's expectations are critical when using shock. Knowing how much shock to use, and when, is a skill. We all have to find our own footing with it. As with any attempt at humor, judging incorrectly can make you feel rejected. With shock, the rejection feels especially harsh, like you've just farted during a book club meeting. Choose wisely, however, and your audience will delight in your rapscallion nature.

Know your audience, be culturally aware, and be perceptive of the standards that govern the platform of your writing, conversation, or performance. Start mild. If your tastes run toward extremely shocking humor, it's best to ramp up to such extremes. Think of entertaining an audience with extremely shocking humor like wooing a date. You start light, with flirtatious innuendo and suggestion. Only once you have buy-in do you progress to the really dirty stuff.

At the time of this writing, society's pendulum, at least in the West, has swung far in the direction of political correctness. Certain words that aren't swear words but that slur, trigger, misidentify, or otherwise disrespect certain oppressed minorities have become taboo and far more shocking than traditional swear words. Unless you have a brilliantly funny idea that can't be expressed without these words, and you can comfort the afflicted and afflict the comfortable, be prepared for a backlash if you decide to use them.

Shock with Your Message

One way to make shock more palatable to a wider audience is to use it to convey a particularly intelligent opinion or statement. Introducing shock will heighten your message. It will show your passion for the subject. On a subliminal level, it will communicate to your audience that you're attempting to be amusing. Therefore, they'll likely interpret your slightly shocking statement as humor, and you'll have a good chance of creating amusement if not outright laughs.

There are occasions when you might want to be extremely shocking for effect. If your message itself is shocking, the shock funny filter is sometimes the most appropriate vehicle. Funny filters can also serve as symbols of your message.

Shock Humor for Kids

Compared to the other funny filters, shock has a unique relationship with the age of your audience. On the one hand, those who profess to be the guardians of chaste society are quick to propose barring children from potential exposure to any shocking material. They label it *adults only*. On the other hand, much of the humor that we traditionally call *shocking* is of particular interest to children. Potty humor, cartoonish violence, swearing, and bodily function humor delight children from a young age. Classic nursery rhymes are filled with dreadful violence. Children use age-appropriate violent stories to process the unimagined horrors that haunt their nightmares. Their humor can serve the same purpose.

The arbitrary decision to make certain words "dirty" has not stopped TikTok videos of young children – sometimes babies – swearing a blue streak from becoming wildly popular, a trend kicked off by Will Ferrell and Adam McKay's *The Landlord* in the early days of online video. As a society, we seem to finally be saying, "What's the harm? They're just words." This is especially true of words for things that are already a regular part of children's lives: poop, pee, and so on. Let them have their fun. Prudish restrictions on their behavior, which only make them want to use forbidden words and talk about forbidden subjects more, are probably a more deeply corrupting influence than the words and subjects themselves. With humor, we have an opportunity to destigmatize and normalize age-appropriate yet shocking subjects to give kids all the benefits of humor: joy, connection, community, and a defense mechanism against life's terrors and anxieties.

Shock Examples

In prose and visual arts, the most famous consistent example of shock is *National Lampoon*, the successful magazine that had its heyday in the 1970s. On screens, the TV shows *Family Guy* and *It's Always Sunny in Philadelphia* revel in shock. In stand-up comedy, you're unlikely to find a single more overtly shocking comedian over the last 30 years than Doug Stanhope. Howard Stern, though recently tamed due to age and his newfound position in the media establishment, was for decades radio's number one "shock jock."

Best Practices

- Swear, offend, and make any reference to sex, drugs, violence, or a host of any "inappropriate" subjects to make humor, and you're using the shock funny filter.
- To make shock accessible to all audiences, use it in moderation.
- Shock works especially well when your underlying message is both interesting and shocking.

Exercises

1. If you're accustomed to using shock humor and enjoy being overtly shocking, try to scale it back so you use it in moderation.
2. If you tend to avoid shock humor, try injecting a small dash of it for emphasis (and fun).

CHAPTER

13

A Hilarious Parody

Parody might seem like a funny filter we can use only if we're producing a full-on sketch, TV show, or movie. Happily, this is not the case. Parody can be used in every medium, including the written word, stand-up, and casual conversation.

When you mimic an established piece or form of entertainment or information, you engage the parody funny filter. Any show, movie, or speech – even a blender instruction manual – can be parodied. Mimicry doesn't necessarily mean mockery, though the funniest parodies often do both.

Most parodies are done in the same format as the work being parodied, though this is not a requirement of the funny filter. Parody of any media can be dropped into conversation.

117

You can parody a movie or TV show by quoting a character from either. You can parody a piece of writing or any other media by simply aping its style or language in a way the reader notices.

What makes parody humorous to audiences is the recognition they experience when they see something they know being referenced, commented on, or mocked. People love seeing familiar entertainment or information spoofed. Parody is so effective in humor that sometimes people enjoy it even if they don't know the source material.

How Parody Works

Parody is an easy funny filter to use. Any mimicry of a form of information or entertainment, especially one your audience recognizes, will spark humor. Adding mockery on top of mimicry makes humor almost inevitable.

Specifically, take a show or movie (or blender instruction manual) and make fun of it. Imitate the form, tone, acting, music, wording, or whatever part of it you choose to accentuate, but make the content your own. Incorporate your own message into the parody. The parody funny filter borrows the structure of something else and lets you re-create the content.

You can parody particular shows, movies, or writing. You can also parody an overall media or format. Nothing need be safe from your ridicule.

You can use parody to mock a specific work, or you can use parody as a format to communicate a message unrelated to the target of your mockery. The latter approach adds humor to an on-the-nose message. Example: you can turn an everyday grocery list into a magazine cover:

One cliché to look out for in parody is fairytales. Fairytale parodies almost never work, partly because fairytales are ancient, and partly because they've been parodied endlessly. As with any cliché, people are tired of them, even if they don't realize it.

Parody Examples

SNL features parodies on every show, almost always an ad, and sometimes a TV show or movie in a sketch. Weird Al Yankovic parodies songs, as well as the biopic format in his movie, *Weird: The Al Yankovic Story*. *The Onion* parodies a news organization.

Doug Kenney and Henry Beard wrote a popular parody of *Lord of the Rings* called *Bored of the Rings*. *MAD* magazine parodies movies and TV shows in comic-book format.

Types of Parody

Writing, TV, and movies are the media most often parodied. But don't let that tendency limit you. You can parody an old radio comedy show by presenting material with cheesy music, stagy performances, and boxy live-audience laughs like Albert Brooks did in his album *A Star Is Bought*. You can parody a conspiracy theory or protest movement like *Birds Aren't Real* does. You can parody internet how-to videos like Fatal Farm did with *Mark's Infinite Solutions*. You can parody a video game, a cereal box, a real estate listing, or even (I'm still waiting) a blender instruction manual.

In the last 50 years, advertising has been the most popular format to parody. We've all seen ad parodies on TV shows, even in movies. You can do it, too. If you imitate the language we typically hear in ads, the parody funny filter will work for you. You can parody a specific ad, an ad genre, or the idea of ads in general. Audiences never tire of ad parodies. They've resisted becoming clichés, probably because we're inundated by thousands of advertising messages every day, keeping them forever relevant.

Parody becomes funnier the closer the mimicry recalls the source material. If you parody something in casual conversation, try to get the voices and delivery as close as you can. If you parody something in writing, make it look like the source material, with the same format, fonts, and design. If video is your medium, ape the production value of the source material as best you can, budget permitting.

Mimicry comes in many forms, from the simple to the sophisticated. One of the simplest parodies I've seen recently was a tweeted photo of a perfect re-creation of the United Artists logo captured in the cast of a shadow across the toilet of an airplane bathroom. The surprising verisimilitude was funny.

Impressions

Imitating another person is the most elemental and perhaps easiest form of parody, especially in casual conversation. You don't have to be good at impressions to create a winning parody. It may be obvious to point out that an impression of someone will be funnier if it's more accurate, but it's not as simple as that. Parody can also be funny if its mimicry faithfully recalls the source material in a fun or creative way. Dana Carvey isn't an accurate impressionist, but his impressions always kill. Audiences love how he captures something recognizable in each voice: a certain turn of phrase, a way of cocking the head, or a certain vocal quirk. It's this spark of recognition that creates the magic of parody.

Best Practices

- If you mimic or mock any form of entertainment or information, you're making use of the parody funny filter.
- Borrow the form or format from your target, but replace the content with your own.

- The better you can spark recognition of your source material, the funnier your parody will be.

Exercises

1. In conversation, next time you want to say something, say it in the voice of a character from a TV show or movie, or parody a famous speech or quote from a movie by twisting the words to match your message.
2. In writing, mimic the style of another kind of writing you like or a kind you don't like.
3. Produce a parody sketch mimicking your favorite TV show or movie.

CHAPTER

14

So Much Hyperbole

Hyperbole is an easy funny filter to explain, but one of the most difficult to execute, even for the professional humorist.

You probably already know that hyperbole means exaggeration. However, just plain exaggeration doesn't necessarily lead to laugh-inducing humor. To give the hyperbole funny filter the fuel it needs, an exaggeration must be so heightened that it violates the rules of reality. This is easier said than done.

Hyperbole requires a message with a value judgment or a statement of quantity, volume, or something else that can be exaggerated. The dry, unfiltered message "I need to go to the store" is more difficult to exaggerate than "The store is too far away." The latter contains a clear quantity that you can exaggerate.

How Hyperbole Works

To get to the essence of what you're working with when you use hyperbole, pretend you're in the audience of *The Tonight Show with Johnny Carson*, which had a long-standing tradition involving hyperbole. When Johnny would say in his opening monologue that it was a hot day in Burbank, the audience would say, "How hot was it?" And they would wait with great anticipation to hear Johnny's hyperbole joke:

"I saw a fire hydrant flagging down a dog," Johnny would say, invoking the hyperbole funny filter by exaggerating to a point of impossibility. A fire hydrant can't flag down a dog, so the hyperbole worked, and got a big laugh.

Find the "how" question in your statement. "How much do you need to go to the grocery store?" The answer will spur hyperbole jokes: "I need to get to the grocery store before I eat another pair of shoes." Or, to add the irony funny filter, "I'm well-stocked. I have a box of mac & cheese that expired in 2008."

What does it mean to exaggerate beyond the bounds of reality? It means a hyperbole should be physically impossible.

You can hyperbolize just about any thought (read on for examples), but beginners might want to start with simple volume-related thoughts like how long something takes, how cold or hot it is, how big or small something is, or something similar that provides an obvious value judgment.

To create hyperbole requires imagination. It requires thinking outside the bounds of the everyday, the possible, and the expected. It's through this beyond-the-everyday scale that the hyperbole funny filter achieves the surprise necessary for humor.

Hyperbole Examples

On stage, every professional stand-up comedian uses the hyperbole funny filter. There's a hyperbolic beat, punchline, or tag in almost every bit. Here, Tig Notaro uses hyperbole to describe how small a town is: "Everybody in this town knows this is not really a town. You're gathering in groups, you're making Aunt Mary the mayor. But no one's falling for it."

In literature and radio drama, Douglas Adams filled his *Hitchhiker's Guide to the Galaxy* series with hyperbole, weaving the impossible and the incongruent into almost every line to communicate the vast scope of the universe and its contents:

- Infinite improbability drive, the incomprehensible technology that allowed for faster-than-light-speed travel through space
- A scientist so focused on useless research that he spent eight years trying to extract sunbeams from cucumbers
- An illness so rare it only affects people who don't have it

HBO's *Mr. Show with Bob and David* excelled at hyperbole. In their sketch "Titannica," a heavy metal band visits a sick kid in a hospital who was so inspired by their "Try Suicide" song that he dove into a vat of acid, reducing his body to a comically impossible, burnt stick figure.

Hyperbole Pitfalls

A common pitfall with hyperbole is not exaggerating enough. It's easy to exaggerate a little, and you may even amuse people with a lot of exaggeration, but to give your humor the best chance to succeed, you have to exaggerate more than you think is possible.

Another pitfall is overthinking. If you use hyperbole to create a concept that's too complicated or too removed from people's experience or understanding, they'll have to work too hard to grasp your exaggeration. Whenever an audience realizes they have to work too hard to understand humor, they immediately give up on it. It's therefore the humorist's job to ensure the humor is easy to understand, easy to follow, and easy to enjoy.

Hyperbole can be used to exaggerate small as well as big. A common hyperbole cliché occurs when someone says they liked a show, book, album, or some other entertainment product, and the creator of the work responds, "Oh, so you're the one?" As with any funny filter, clichés are always a pitfall to watch out for.

Setting Up Hyperbole

Hyperbole needs context to work. The audience needs a set-up for the hyperbole punchline. If Johnny Carson said only the punchline of the fire hydrant/dog joke, no one would understand it. In some circumstances, you can assume your audience knows the context. If they don't, you can give it to them in a subtle way, like integrating it into your hyperbolic comment. Or you can give it to them in an obvious way, as overt exposition. Johnny Carson used the latter method, setting it up plainly by stating, "It was so hot in Burbank today . . ."

If you're in a traffic jam, you and the other passengers in your car have the same context, and you can make a hyperbolic comment without mentioning how slow the traffic is moving. You just have to think of ways to hyperbolize the slow-moving traffic by coming up with an impossible explanation. One possibility: "I can't tell if this is traffic or God ceasing the forward motion of time."

Dry, non-humorous statements such as "I like cake," "I need to be at work by 9 a.m.," "I'm reading a good book," and "I don't like when you do that" can all be hyperbolized.

Can you find the value judgment in each statement? Look for the part you can hyperbolize. I like cake – how much do you like it? What is an impossible way to describe it? Do you like cake so much that you can't believe there's still cake left on earth during your lifetime?

Coming up with a good hyperbole joke can be stressful. You'll probably feel some performance anxiety or even full-blown stage fright in the process. Remember to try your best, have fun, and keep trying. If you fail, make a joke about how you failed (see the metahumor funny filter in Chapter 19).

Hyperbole can be made somewhat easier and more fun with a partner. When someone makes a hyperbole joke to you, you can respond by accepting the new temporary reality they established with their hyperbole, and then hyperbolize it further. "What is this 'cake' concept you speak of? Tales are told of this once-abundant dessert item before you, the great cake eater, were born." Now you're riffing. You've turned a regular exchange into an improv jam.

I NOW ENTER THE HYPERBOLIC CHAMBER AND WILL EMERGE IN 10 BILLION YEARS

Best Practices

- The hyperbole funny filter makes statements humorous when you exaggerate beyond the physically possible.

- You can use hyperbole to create humor out of anything that's quantifiable: amounts, sizes, intensities, and more.

Exercises

1. When you have something superlative to say, try to hyperbolize it by exaggerating it to an impossible extreme. You'll likely be disappointed in your first efforts. Have fun and keep trying.
2. Write a list of 10 hyperbolic ways to express an idea. You might be pleasantly surprised to find at least one of them humorous.

15

Playing with Words

Words sometimes sound like other words. They sometimes have the same meanings but are spelled differently. Sometimes, they're spelled the same but pronounced differently. With words like these in the complicated and messy English language, such inconsistencies can all be exploited for humor. Puns, made-up words, interesting or unusual groupings of words, and word repetition can all work to create humor.

How Wordplay Works

The wordplay funny filter is exactly what it says it is. It's playing with words, particularly in ways different from their official or traditional use.

If the funny filters are toys, wordplay is the barrel of monkeys, and there are many, many monkeys to play with. When you use wordplay and use it well, people will not only think you're funny, they'll think you're smart. Wordplay is frequently the realm of high-IQ humorists who like word puzzles and brain games. Comedian Demetri Martin uses a lot of advanced wordplay, often layered on top of other wordplay. He once told a joke that was a lengthy palindrome.

Wordplay Devices

In the interest of completeness, here is an exhaustive list of each named wordplay device, divided into two categories: ones that will likely work to create humor, and ones that will likely leave people scratching their heads.

Wordplay Devices That Work to Create Humor

- **Anagram:** rearranging the letters of a word or phrase to produce a new word or phrase

- **Blanagram:** rearranging the letters of a word or phrase and substituting one single letter to produce a new word or phrase

- **Janusism:** the use of phonetics to create a humorous word or part of a word

- **Malapropism:** incorrect use of a word by substituting a similar-sounding word with different meaning

- **Mondegreen:** a mishearing (usually unintentional) of a homophone or lyric that, as a result, acquires a new meaning

- **Neologism:** a newly created word

- **Onomatopoeia:** a word or grouping of words that imitates the sound it's describing

- **Oronyms:** homophones of multiple words or phrases

- **Oxymoron:** a combination of two contradictory terms

- **Paraprosdokian:** a sentence whose latter part is surprising or unexpected in a way that causes the reader or listener to reframe the first

- **Portmanteau:** a new word that fuses two words or morphemes

- **Pun:** deliberate use of two similar-sounding words as one word

- **Rebus:** a code in which pictures and math represent sounds or words to be decoded

- **Rhyme:** matching words that sound alike (best used in lyrics as opposed to prose)

- **Spoonerism:** a switch of two sounds in two different words

- **Tongue twisters:** words that are difficult to say together
- **Word repetition:** use of a word as many times as possible within a single line or joke
- **Word switch:** swapping two words in a sentence
- **Zeugma:** the use of a single phrase in two ways simultaneously

Wordplay Devices Best Avoided in Humor

- **Acronym:** abbreviations formed by combining the initial letters in a phrase
- **Acrostic:** the first letter, syllable or word of each line arranged to spell out a new message
- **Alliteration:** matching sounds at the beginning of words
- **Ambigram:** a word that can be read mirrored or upside down
- **Ananym:** a name with reversed letters of another name
- **Antigram:** an anagram that means the opposite of the original phrase
- **Apronym:** an acronym that's also a phrase pertaining to the original meaning
- **Aptronym:** a name that aptly represents a person or character
- **Assonance:** matching vowel sounds
- **Auto-antonym:** a word that contains opposite meanings
- **Autogram:** a sentence that provides an inventory of its own characters

- **Backronym:** a phrase back-formed by treating a word that's originally not an initialism or acronym as one
- **Caesar shift:** moving all the letters in a word or sentence some fixed number of positions down the alphabet
- **Charactonym:** a name that suggests the personality traits of a fictional character
- **Chinglish:** a blend of Mandarin and English – a stereotype that should be avoided
- **Chronogram:** a phrase or sentence in which some letters can be interpreted as numerals and rearranged to stand for a particular date
- **Consonance:** matching consonant sounds
- **Conversion (word formation):** a transformation of a word of one word class into another word class
- **Dog Latin:** a debased form of Latin
- **Eponym:** applying a person's name to a place
- **Euphemism:** intentionally using a word or phrase with a more polite tone over one with a harsher tone
- **Gramogram:** a word or sentence in which the names of the letters or numerals are used to represent the word
- **Holorime:** a rhyme that encompasses an entire line or phrase
- **Homograph:** words with the same spellings but with different meanings (okay when used as a pun)
- **Homonym:** words with the same sounds and same spellings but with different meanings (okay when used as a pun)
- **Homophone:** words with the same sounds but with different meanings

- **Homophonic translation:** phonetically spelling out words from another language

- **Interlanguages, mixed languages, and macaronic languages:** mingling words and phrases from different languages

- **Jumble:** a word game in which the solution of a puzzle is its anagram

- **Kenning:** use of a large number of words to say what could be said with fewer

- **Lallation:** when *l* is pronounced *r*

- **Language game:** a system of manipulating spoken words to render them incomprehensible to the untrained ear

- **Letter bank:** using the letters from a certain word or phrase as many times as wanted to produce a new word or phrase

- **Lipogram:** writing in which a certain letter or letters are missing

- **Mesostic:** writing in which a vertical phrase intersects lines of horizontal text

- **Mnemonic:** a device such as a pattern of letters, ideas, or associations that assists in remembering something

- **Palindrome:** a word or phrase that reads the same in either direction

- **Pangram:** a sentence that uses every letter of the alphabet at least once

- **Phonetic reversal:** the process of reversing the phonemes or phones of a word or phrase

- **Phono-semantic matching:** The borrowing of a word into one language from another, completely or partially preserving both the original sound and meaning
- **Pig Latin:** a secret language formed from English by transferring the initial consonant or consonant cluster of each word to the end of the word and adding the syllable -*ay*
- **RAS syndrome:** repetition of a word by using it both as a word alone and as a part of an acronym
- **Recursive acronym:** an acronym that has the acronym itself as one of its components
- **Replacement backronym:** a phrase back-formed from an existing initialism or acronym that is originally an abbreviation with another meaning
- **Retronym:** creating a new word to denote an old object or concept whose original name has come to be used for something else
- **Slang:** the use of informal words or expressions
- **Sobriquet:** a popularized nickname
- **Sub-alphabetic words:** words derived from only using part of the alphabet
- **Tautogram:** a phrase or sentence in which every word starts with the same letter
- **Tmesis:** the separation of parts of a compound word by an intervening word or words, heard mainly in informal speech
- **Tom Swifty:** a quote ascribed to Tom, followed by an adverb linked to the quote

- **Typewriter words:** words that can only be spelled with letters from the top row of the typewriter
- **Ubbi dubbi:** a language game in which players insert "ub" before the vowels in words; variations of Ubbi Dubbi include Obbish, Ob, Ib, Arpy Darpy, and Iz
- **Univocalic:** poetry that uses only one vowel
- **Wellerism:** a quote and attribution with an added clause that analogizes or contradicts the quote
- **Word square:** a series of letters arranged in the form of a square that could be read both vertically and horizontally

Maybe you can invent a new way to play with words that's not on this list.

Despite my earlier warning about the effectiveness of the wordplay devices on the second list, there are no hard rules in humor, only suggested guidelines. Use some of these more obscure wordplay devices if you like. Just be prepared for the uphill battle to connect with your audience.

There's one place where all wordplay devices can be used, and that's when they're couched in the metahumor funny filter (see Chapter 19). Monty Python made good use of several in "The Man Who Speaks in Anagrams," "Dinsdale," and many other sketches.

Popular Wordplay Devices

Two of the most popular wordplay devices are rhymes and puns.

Most of us remember rhyme as our earliest encounter with the wordplay funny filter. We can often summon or at least notice rhyming words when we're in a conversation. If you're writing, composing rhymes is as easy as thumbing through online rhyming dictionaries. Aside from its use in serious poems, children's books, and lyrics, rhyming tickles people and primes them for humor. Rhyming is like the training-wheels wordplay device that prepares both humorists and audiences for more advanced devices like puns, made-up words, and portmanteau.

Puns are one of the easiest wordplay devices to explore. If done right, they're generally successful in creating humor. To make your own puns, start with a set of homographs or homophones and see what happens when you switch words around or use them in a sentence so that either word definition results in a coherent sentence. If the sentence is coherent with only one definition of the word but not both, it will likely receive groans rather than laughs.

Examples:

"If you can think of a better fish pun . . . let minnow."

This pun doesn't work because it only makes sense if you interpret *minnow* as *me know*. It doesn't make sense if you interpret *minnow* as the fish.

"I'm friends with 25 letters of the alphabet. I don't know why."

This pun works because the sentence makes sense if you interpret *why* as *why*, and it makes sense if you interpret *why* as *Y*.

It may be difficult for you to think of puns or other wordplay words off the cuff. Wordplay such as this is more easily done in prose.

Other wordplay devices worth exploring are neologisms, word switches, and word repetition.

Making up words is fun. If you haven't done it, try it some time. You can make up an onomatopoeia, a compound word, or just a word that seems to make sense. George Carlin was fond of making up new compound words in his act. Comedian Rich Hall made a career of neologisms with his *Sniglets*. If you encounter a thing that doesn't have a name, give it one.

Word switches can also be fun. Start with a sentence of your own or with a popular saying or truism. If you replace a key word in the sentence with a similar word, what happens? If you replace a word with a wildly out-of-place word, what happens? Try a few and see if you can come up with something amusing.

Word repetition is a great way to squeeze a laugh out of someone. Can you make up a sentence that uses the same word four or five times? That's a good achievement and can be a source for humor. You've noticed that words start to sound like nonsense when they're repeated enough times. This effect also activates the madcap funny filter (Chapter 16).

THE HUMOR MAGAZINE ACCEPTED MY CRYPTOGRAM! BUT THEY'RE PAYING ME IN CHRONOGRAMS

Of course, the above is just a start. All wordplay is enhanced if other funny filters are also at play.

Wordplay Examples

Some of the best consistent wordplay on screens at the time of this writing is in the monologue of *Jimmy Kimmel Live*. Find his routines online to see his master writers at work.

Children's books, joke books, and Laffy Taffy packages are great sources for puns and other wordplay. Notice how many of the puns in these sources only work with one meaning of the word and not the other.

The wordplay used by Del Close in his bit part in *Ferris Bueller's Day Off* is unique. He doesn't so much play with the words as with the pauses between, drawing out the space so agonizingly that we can feel the crushing boredom he inflicts on his students.

Best Practices

- Create humor using the wordplay funny filter by using words in ways they aren't intended.

- There are dozens of different wordplay devices, most of which will confuse and confound audiences. For the best results, stick to those in the "Wordplay Devices That Work to Create Humor" list.

- When creating a pun, be sure your sentence makes sense no matter which way your audience interprets the word.

Exercises

1. Play with words, both verbally and in your writing.
2. Try switching words around to see how it affects meaning.
3. Make up new words for ideas, actions, or objects that don't have a name.
4. See if you can express your message with a sentence that uses one of the many wordplay devices.

CHAPTER

16

Getting Carried Away

Madcap is the funny filter most people stop using when they grow up, and when they do, part of the magic of childhood is lost. Those lucky few who continue to use madcap as adults sip from the fountain of youth. Madcap inspires a sense of silliness. In order to use it, you have to stop caring how stupid you look, which can be freeing.

Performing madcap, or using it in daily life, is magic, but you don't have to be a clown to enjoy it. Even those too shy or austere to use it themselves can benefit just from being in the audience when others use it. When we laugh at the antics of a madcap story or performance, we laugh with abandon and feel young again.

How Madcap Works

The madcap funny filter is present when anything silly, nonsensical, goofy, or physical happens. Standing funny, walking funny, or moving funny in any way can spark madcap humor. Wearing silly hats or oversized (or undersized) clothes also counts as madcap. If you dare to use the madcap funny filter, you turn your physical space, your body, or the body of your characters into living comedy.

Madcap is easy to use, and anyone can do it, but most of us have a block. Breaking through this block isn't easy. We all want to be perceived as cool and collected adults, not goofballs. We want our message to be taken seriously. But this buttoned-up attitude is hamstringing our ability to use the madcap funny filter to create humor. We're afraid it will make us look foolish. It will indeed, and that's what makes it funny. Remember that a message delivered with humor – even madcap humor – is always more memorable.

We may not remember what US presidents say, but we always remember when they wander aimlessly, walk with toilet paper stuck to their shoe, or fall down.

We enjoy madcap humor because it enables us to relate to someone's physical pain or discomfort without experiencing it (the benign violation theory, described in Chapter 2). It helps us deal with the pain of life. Even babies laugh when people fall and make funny faces. It's inherent in almost everyone's sense of humor. A funny face is different and unexpected, another iteration of the game of peekaboo. We enjoy seeing a face we know and love become a different face and then return to normal.

Madcap Examples

George Carlin and Steve Martin are taken very seriously, often ranked among the greatest comic geniuses of the twentieth century. What people forget is that they were masters of the unserious madcap funny filter. They acted like fools, made goofy faces, funny sounds, and spouted a lot of nonsense.

Madcap has largely fallen out of favor in modern American stand-up comedy. Surprisingly, many stand-up comics don't use this high-leverage tool. They stand with blank stares and recite their jokes while remaining as still and expressionless as possible. However, if you watch history's most successful stand-up comics, you'll see they make wild, funny gestures and facial expressions throughout their acts.

The British have a reputation for being more adept at madcap than Americans. Monty Python's "Ministry of Silly Walks" sketch is a prime example. In prose, *Private Eye* magazine and the novels of Leonard Wibberly, Douglas Adams, and Maeve Higgins shine in prose. English comedian Stewart Lee braves silly noises and physicality in his act to a degree most US comedians would never dare.

On the big screen in recent decades, Jim Carrey and Chris Farley excelled in madcap. *In Living Color, Tim and Eric's Awesome Show Great Job*, and *The Eric Andre Show* brought madcap to the small screen.

How to Use Madcap

To use the madcap funny filter in any medium, allow yourself to play the boob. Welcome people to laugh *at* you. Act like an idiot, make funny faces, speak nonsense words, fall down, and be wacky. You can wear something silly or out of place. You can move your body in a funny, unexpected way. You can say random things that don't make sense and have no relevance to anything.

In prose, you can use nonsense words. You can describe funny sounds, funny faces, funny pratfalls, and other physical humor.

Madcap is a delightful main course in humor. It also makes a nice garnish. Enhance any humor by layering madcap with other funny filters. Most of us have fallen on a slippery surface and know what that's like. If a character stumbles and falls, let's say walking across ice, suddenly you have reference and madcap together.

You can pair madcap with shock to create riotous laughs. This funny filter pairing delivered the biggest laughs in *Some Like It Hot*, *There's Something About Mary*, and *Bridesmaids*.

Madcap works best to communicate an important message. The contrasting of silliness with seriousness adds irony. Madcap with no message, which is silliness for silliness's sake, can feel empty.

Chevy Chase became famous in the first year of *SNL* by playing President Gerald Ford as a bumbling klutz who suffered over-the-top pratfalls. The stunts were memorable in the wake of Watergate, when audiences exhausted by weighty political satire craved comedy that lampooned authority figures, especially the president, in a mindless, silly way instead.

Best Practices

- Tap into the power of the madcap funny filter by daring to be silly.
- Pair madcap with a serious message for maximum effect.

Exercises

1. Experiment with throwing your face and body into your humor in any way you can to accentuate what you have to say. Be nonsensical.
2. In writing, try to paint a picture of physical humor.

17

A Good Analogy

Alot of "how to write humor" books and articles will tell you to find two disparate things and put them together. There are even books about creativity that say the essence of artistic invention is to put two things together that have never been out together before. This is the basis of the analogy funny filter.

Let's do a test. Take four coins of various denominations and lay them on a table top. How would you define the relationship between the coins? If you say, "They're all money," "They're all round," and "They're all metallic," you're a person who tends to see the relationship between things in terms of their similarities.

If, however, you say, "They're all different amounts," and "Some are bronze and some are silver," then you're a person who tends to see the relationship between things in terms of their differences.

You may be flexible, without a strong tendency one way or the other.

The thinking you brought to this little test is the same thinking required to use the analogy funny filter. Whether you're adept at seeing the similarities between things or putting two mismatched things together, you can use either skill to create humor using analogy.

How Analogy Works

If you remember from high school the difference between a simile and an analogy, where similes use *like* or *as* when comparing two things, and analogies directly equate two things without *like* or *as*, never mind that. The particular use of conjunctions is a minor detail that needn't concern the humorist. The analogy funny filter covers both concepts.

Analogy works to make an audience link two unrelated things that they might not think to compare otherwise, which can be fun, like a connect-the-dots game. Each new point of comparison the humorist makes between the two things can spark a laugh.

The analogy funny filter is an easy one to use. Most of us can compare two things, either physical or conceptual. Comparing, for example, your family to a rock band, the current political situation to a doomsday cult, or the service in a restaurant to a criminal autopsy can result in a lot of humor.

How to Use Analogy

To start, make a list of pairs of disparate things that have similarities. Start with things in your life or things associated with your message. The more unrelated the pair, the better your chances of achieving humor. For example, you could compare reading to a coma: "Reading a book is like being in a coma. You're sitting there a really long time. You're not moving. People talk to you, but you don't hear what they're saying because you're lost in your head. Your spouse eventually leaves you for someone who likes to get out more."

When you can find several details that can apply to both things, you know you've found a fruitful analogy.

However, let's say you want to compare shirts and pants: "Did you ever notice that shirts and pants are similar? You put both of them on your body. You want them both to fit." The analogy doesn't work because shirts and pants are too similar. They give you no space to play. They have no contrast. Contrast introduces irony, and irony helps the audience identify the game.

Here are some examples of disparate pairings that might make good analogies:

- A cold sales call analogized with trying to coax a cat out from under a bed
- A birdwatcher analogized with a peeping Tom

- Taking care of a baby analogized with having a drug addiction
- Stopping for gas analogized with robbing a stagecoach

Simply comparing two things is the simplest form of analogy and only the beginning of an attempt at humor. To get laughs, analogy has to proceed to the next step, which is called *mapping*.

Mapping borrows the reference funny filter to find relatable or known features of one of the paired items and applies them to the other. In the reading/coma example, traits common to reading are applied, or "mapped" onto being in a coma, and they get more absurd as they progress.

A Hidden Message

When making a humorous analogy, you can use *like* or *as* for a simple, one-line joke ("Birdwatching is like being a peeping Tom"). You can also extend the observation and map one of the two things being compared onto the other. The most humorous way to do this is to conceal one thing from the audience and only allude to it. This kind of prolonged analogy creates a hidden message in the humor, a layered game of peekaboo.

Let's say you came up with a comparison you like: running into someone you know at the grocery store analogized with encountering a grizzly bear in the woods.

This comparison alone contains plenty of the reference and irony funny filters (as well as misplaced focus, Chapter 18), so it alone might get some laughs. But let's say you wanted to expand the joke using mapping. You would start by looking for commonalities between the two experiences:

- You feel a flood of panic.
- You hope you brought your spray.
- You make yourself larger to repel the individual.
- Maybe playing dead is the best strategy, so you just slump over your cart in the health food aisle.
- Don't climb a tree – the grocery store acquaintance is likely to chase you up there and make small talk.

Each connection you make that your audience recognizes as applying to the hidden part of the analogy (in this case, the bear encounter) will result in a spark of humor.

Analogy Examples

Chris Rock made an excellent short analogy, comparing police officers to airline pilots:

> I know it's hard being a cop, but some jobs can't have "bad apples." Some jobs, everybody's got to be good. Like pilots. American Airlines can't be like, "Most of our pilots like to land. We just got a few bad apples that like to crash into mountains."

In an excellent example of mapping, "The Barber" episode of *Seinfeld* analogizes getting a new barber to having an affair.

George Carlin offers a master-level example of the analogy funny filter in his "Football/Baseball" bit. It begins with several examples of expert mapping, culminating with a long comparison:

> The object of the game in football is for the quarterback, otherwise known as the field general, to be on target with his aerial assault, riddling the defense by hitting his receivers with deadly accuracy in spite of the blitz, even if he has to use the shotgun. With short bullet passes and long bombs, he marches his troops into enemy territory, balancing this aerial assault with a sustained ground attack which punches holes in the forward wall of the enemy's defensive line.
>
> In baseball, the object is to go home!

However, the comparison between football and baseball is not the analogy. Football and baseball, like shirts and pants, are too similar.

Where Carlin uses analogy is how he defines each sport. He analogizes football to war and baseball to kids playing in a yard. By making one sport the war-like activity and the other a safe triviality, he creates irony by comparing two different analogies. This is an example of how the funny filters can be combined and played with in creative ways.

Best Practices

- Use analogy to compare two disparate things. Sometimes the comparison alone will register as a joke to your audience.

- To expand your analogy, find specific similarities between the two things. Each similarity you uncover creates a new joke.

- Throughout the string of jokes in a longer analogy, refer to one of the two things overtly while keeping the other hidden.

- Use mapping to apply recognizable features of one onto the other.

Exercises

1. Practice finding similarities among unrelated things. In casual conversation, try to think of things that are analogous to any aspect of your message.
2. On stage or in the written word, expound on your favorite analogies by mapping the features of one onto the other to show several points of comparison.

18

Misplaced Focus

An important element in more advanced versions of the peekaboo game is the humorist's lack of awareness, touched on in Chapter 9. Among all the funny filters, misplaced focus highlights this element best of all. Here, the humorist pretends not to notice the most obvious thing. It could be a fatal flaw, some aspect of your message, or a key detail. In any instance, when you use misplaced focus skillfully, you compel the audience to spot the very thing you appear to be ignoring.

How Misplaced Focus Works

The misplaced focus funny filter can be used in many different ways to make many different kinds of jokes. In each, the audience's focus is directed to the wrong thing, the unfunny thing, the uninteresting thing. They'll play along with this diversion, understanding that there's an elephant in the room that you don't want them to see. Using misplaced focus is like telling people, "Don't think of the elephant," which, of course, is exactly what they'll do.

How to Use Misplaced Focus

Misplaced focus dances around the elephant in the room, or whatever obvious thing the humorist has chosen to ignore, getting as close to mentioning it as possible without actually doing so.

One way you can use the misplaced focus funny filter is through misdirection. This is a common joke structure used in a lot of stand-up comedy. It's even become somewhat of a clichéd joke structure in recent years.

In conversation, pretending not to notice something particularly noticeable can be funny, especially if you make comments about things other than the noticeable thing, as if you're unaware of it. This can be as unsophisticated as combining madcap and mild shock by having a conversation while a chunk of food is stuck to your mouth, or as sophisticated as praising a work of art, referencing obscure details about art history, pretending not to notice that the work of art you're reviewing at is hanging at Denny's.

Pretending to be oblivious to your intentions or your message highlights what you have to say. This not only helps get your message across, it does it with humor.

In writing, you have even more opportunities to take advantage of misplaced focus. You can use the same one-line jokes as in stand-up. You can also prolong the game and extend your lack of awareness by using misplaced focus as a structure for a longer piece of comedic writing, like an essay about neglecting to care for your yard that ignores the fact that your house is submerged under 20 feet of seawater.

This funny filter works particularly well with subjects that are politically charged, controversial, or that inflame the passions of your audience. It's a prolonged tease where you extend the game of peekaboo and refuse to reveal your face for an agonizingly long time, in some cases never revealing it, but making the baby uncover it on their own.

Misplaced Focus Examples

The movie *Get Out* is rife with misplaced focus humor. One instance concerns the McGuffin, which is kept concealed for most of the movie. Another is the comic relief character, Rod, who consistently focuses on wrong and unimportant things: his TSA work, which he considers to be extremely important, his idea that he should have been the protagonist's girlfriend's pick, and his mistaken idea that the mystery plot involves turning Black people into sex slaves.

Stand-up comedian Anthony Jeselnik is a master of the one-line misdirect. You hear it in almost every one of his jokes:

> In a bar fight, your fists will only take you so far. At some point you have to break a bottle in half. Your opponent will put up their hands and say, "whoa." And the only thing you can say is, "do not bring a fist to a glass bottle fight, Mom."

In literature, Jonathon Swift's *A Modest Proposal* is the most classic example of misplaced focus. To raise awareness of starving children in Ireland, he proposes a ridiculous solution: eating them. He spends most of the essay describing delicious children-centered recipes.

The Onion uses misplaced focus frequently in its parody news articles:

- Dazed Jeff Bezos Realizes He Spent Entire Conversation Thinking About How to Automate Person Talking to Him
- New Study Finds Humans Experience Greatest Feelings of Joy When Pushing 'Skip Ad' Button
- CIA Realizes It's Been Using Black Highlighters All These Years

Best Practices

- By shifting focus away from the obvious and onto something trivial, you engage the misplaced focus funny filter to create humor.

- Use misplaced focus to raise awareness of your message by pretending to ignore it.

Exercises

1. Think of an obvious or inept way you can obscure your message. Come up with tangential but related things you can talk about that dance around your message as if you're unaware of what your message is.

2. Practice this prolonged lack of awareness until you understand just how close you have to dance around your message in order for people to add two and two and understand that you're hiding your face from them in a grown-up version of peekaboo.

CHAPTER

19

Going Meta

What do you think of humor? Do you like it? Do some attempts at humor annoy you? What makes some things funny and other things not? Your answers to these questions will lead to metahumor.

Metahumor can seem tricky or highfalutin to the uninitiated. If you're intimidated by the concept, rest assured that metahumor, like all the funny filters, can be used to create humor that's dumb and simple just as easily as it can create humor that's intellectual and sophisticated.

In its most sophisticated form, metahumor can confound and sometimes anger audiences and even some humorists. It's experimental comedy performed for niche audiences who love to argue about what's funny and what's not. In its simplest form, metahumor is just laughing at yourself, your own jokes, or bad jokes in general.

How Metahumor Works

The metahumor funny filter is engaged whenever a humorist deconstructs or makes fun of other humor, or the idea of humor. It's humor that "breaks the fourth wall" (acknowledging that it's entertainment and removing the barrier between the world of the show and the real world, sometimes by directly addressing the audience). Why do humans laugh? What makes us enjoy humor? Contemplating these questions and articulating your answers, you'll arrive at value judgments and opinions that will give you a great jumping-off point for using metahumor. Run those answers, value judgments, and opinions through one or more of the other funny filters and see what kind of layered humor you can build.

As with most of the funny filters, metahumor can be executed in many ways, from the elemental to the highly advanced. The simplest way to use metahumor is to critique any humor attempt, including your own, using more humor. A joke about yourself trying to make a joke, or someone else trying to make a joke, is metahumor in action.

Audiences delight in the authenticity and humility of a humorist who's self-aware enough to acknowledge a failure to get laughs. They also delight in laughing at someone playing the fool. Everyone can relate to the experience, so it triggers empathy and respect, combining the reference and metahumor funny filters.

Making fun of your own failed jokes using self-deprecating metahumor can become a crutch or, more accurately, a check written from your "confidence account." It will work once or twice if done in a light-hearted manner, and your audience will bond more closely with you and continue to believe you're confident for a time. But if you do it too many times, you'll come across as weak. Worse, if you self-deprecate so much that you reach a level of self-loathing ("I'm terrible at making jokes" or "I'm not funny"), you'll quickly overdraw your account, and the audience will see the telltale signs that you're in a confidence deficit (flop sweat, stuttering, etc.). Any future attempts at humor after such a dip will likely be met with blank stares, evidence that your audience has given up on you.

Building back that confidence capital is some of the most difficult work in comedy. Some comedians put themselves in this deficit on purpose while on stage, setting up a challenge to dig themselves out of their hole and win the audience back. This crucible is an excellent confidence-building exercise.

Metahumor Examples

Metahumor can incorporate any of the other funny filters by critiquing their use. Steve Martin's entire stand-up act used character, parody, madcap, and metahumor. His persona, a clown-bumbling authority archetype, was a parody of stand-up comedy itself. He meant for you to laugh at how his comedy routines – and the idea of comedy performance per se – are ridiculous more than he wanted you to laugh at the jokes themselves.

Andy Daly, star of Comedy Central's *Review* did a stellar parody of a stand-up performance for *Comedy Death Ray*, a master class in metahumor.

In Pixar's *Finding Nemo*, Marlin, the clown fish, is asked by others to tell a joke. They assume he's funny because he's a clown fish. He fumbles through the incompetent telling of a joke, and the other fish are unimpressed. Like many Pixar movies, which do a great service to audiences by delivering stories and humor that appeal to both kids and adults, *Finding Nemo* doesn't disappoint in this scene. Young kids recognize the metahumor inherent in someone telling a bad joke to a stone-faced audience. Slightly older kids understand and enjoy the metahumor and irony of, particularly, a clown fish failing at being a clown. The adults recognize an even deeper layer of metahumor and irony in the fact that the actor voicing the clown fish is none other than Albert Brooks, one of the funniest and most inventive comedians in history.

The Del Close scene from *Ferris Bueller* uses metahumor. The fact that he lectures the students about irony makes it not only ironic but also a comment on irony itself.

How to Use Metahumor

In person, start with self-deprecating humor that makes fun of your own humor. Making fun of someone else's attempt at humor is risky. It can cross over into bullying quickly. However, if you focus on comforting the afflicted and afflicting the comfortable, you can make fun of mainstream comedy to find plenty of good metahumor.

In prose, you can write an essay critiquing humor. If you're a storyteller, you can create characters who try to be funny and fail. You can experiment with characters who deconstruct humor. The same approach works in film and video.

On stage, attempt to rescue a failed joke by commenting on how poorly it went over. This almost always gets a bigger laugh than the original joke. You can heckle yourself the way Jim Gaffigan does, using a character voice to comment on his own act while he performs it.

Explaining why humor is funny or not funny can sometimes be funny in and of itself. If you or someone else makes a joke, whether it's successful or not, trying to break down the reasons why it worked or didn't work like some kind of joke scientist is pure metahumor.

Metahumor Pitfalls

A stand-up comedian's worst nightmare is a heckler who mocks the performance by calling out jokes that are funnier than what's happening on stage. Such a hypothetical heckler would be employing metahumor. If the comedian retorts with the ol' "Why don't you come on stage and try to do this?" routine (not recommended), the comedian deepens the metahumor by turning it on the heckler. Invariably, the heckler will be nervous on stage and fail to perform under the spotlight, completing a little trip down the rabbit hole of metahumor.

Metahumor experiments like this are fun for other comedians to analyze, but generally spoil the fun for most audiences.

As with parody (Chapter 13), audiences enjoy seeing mainstream, popular comedy shows being mocked. But making fun of more sophisticated humor that's respected by sophisticated audiences takes chutzpah. In order to get away with it, you have to be confident that your humor is funnier than the humor you're mocking. Gary Gullman used this kind of metahumor to lay into Jerry Seinfeld in his *Born on Third Base* HBO special.

Andy Kindler is a comedian who's made a career out of tearing down hack entertainment and comedians he finds unfunny, including Bill Maher and Jimmy Fallon, sometimes viciously. He once offered $1 million to anyone who could produce a video in which Whoopi Goldberg was funny. A delight to those who appreciate hard-hitting metahumor, he probably won't be booked on many late-night talk shows anytime soon.

"Dad jokes" are a recent metahumor trend, making fun of the bad jokes dads tell that make kids roll their eyes.

Best Practices

- Make fun of humor, deconstruct it, or comment on it to create metahumor.

- The easiest way to use metahumor is to acknowledge when you fail in an attempt to be funny and then tell a joke about your failure.

Exercises

1. Notice what kind of humor you like and don't like to discover your take on humor.
2. Form an opinion about any kind of humor and articulate it.
3. Run your opinion through some of the other funny filters to see if you arrive at anything humorous.

CHAPTER

20

Putting It All Together

In the game of peekaboo, we hide our face and then reveal it. In the banana-snatching gag, we tempt someone with something and then take it away. You can see the structure of these simple, childlike, and chimplike games in every funny filter. A character puts up a mask and then reveals the humorist's message. Parody shows us what seems like a recognizable production and then takes it away, leaving us with just a spoof. An analogy hides one concept and then reveals it through another. Hyperbole shows us a relatable, quantifiable statement and then takes it away by making it absurd.

In every funny filter, there's an element of the benign violation. There's the element of surprise. These are the things that go into making all humor, from the most basic to the most sophisticated.

Combining Filters

To start, work with one funny filter at a time. Plenty of successful jokes and other attempts at humor have been achieved through the use of only one funny filter, used in its most basic way.

Once you've tried and succeeded to use the funny filters one at a time and you've enjoyed some success, try a few rudimentary pairings. You can combine the funny filters in any way you want. Start with a clear and interesting message, and then start mixing and matching funny filters.

You can also throw every funny filter in a pile and try to use them all at once if you're feeling bold. That works, too. Whatever would be fun for you is fair game in humor.

The funny filters are like notes in the same key. There's no way to make a dissonant chord. You can play and create new notes of humor just like you can play only the black keys on a piano to sound like you know what you're doing.

Here are some other popular pairings worth trying:

- Character, shock, and madcap work well to accentuate and exaggerate a slob archetype by making someone truly disgusting. Melissa McCarthy's character in *Bridesmaids* is a good example, as are most of Chris Farley's characters.

- Reference pairs nicely with hyperbole in stand-up. Comedians often start with a reference and then escalate the joke by hyperbolizing it several times, each joke beat becoming more hyperbolized. They often sprinkle some madcap and shock on top as they roll out the hyperbole jokes.

- Madcap and character can make funny animals talk, the comic fuel behind so many popular animated movies.

- Analogy and misplaced focus are great structural funny filters that can serve as the framework for funny scenes, essays, or articles.

- Madcap and wordplay work together to create irony, madcap being broad and dumb, and wordplay being specific and intellectual. *Sesame Street* often capitalized on this pairing.

- Reference and metahumor can be used to make fun of a humor style or a joke you just told.

Keep Playing

The funny filters are not a formula. They're building blocks. Expressed through your one-of-a-kind voice, they'll create jokes tailor-made for you.

To give your humor the best chance to succeed, keep it simple, say it with confidence, and keep trying. Boost your confidence by trying to write or say funny things without consciously thinking of the funny filters, and then go back and analyze what you wrote to see where you instinctively used them.

One of the easiest mistakes to make in humor is to get ahead of yourself. Complicating humor kills it far more often than you might think. You'll encounter plenty of challenges trying to make people laugh with only one funny filter at a time. You don't need to make things any more difficult for yourself. Few people in your audience can tell the difference between a simple joke and a multilayered one. You're just as likely to get laughs from one as the other. No points are given for difficulty. Simpler is always better, especially if you're just starting out.

You've seen complex suggestions for how to stack, twist, combine, and play with the funny filters in this chapter and others. Aspire to this level of play if you like, but don't let it intimidate you. If you're new to these concepts, be a kid who's come over to my house to play. These toys might be different than the ones you have at your house, and maybe they're exciting because they're new and different. Sure, I might have more experience with them, but we're best friends. You can come over anytime you want, and you can play with any of the toys however you want.

Best Practices

- Combine different funny filters to find new ways to communicate your message humorously.
- Have fun playing and experimenting with the funny filters.

Exercises

1. Look at the exercise you did for Chapter 8. What do you think?
2. Try writing some new jokes without thinking of the funny filters.
3. Assess your jokes and see if you can identify any funny filters used.

21

The Cringe Factor

These days, a lot of people are worried about saying the wrong joke. This is one of the unfortunate modern perils of humor. If you take the advice of the preceding chapters – have fun, read the room, comfort the afflicted and afflict the comfortable, and others – you'll avoid the worst pitfalls in the delicate and politically charged situations we sometimes find ourselves in.

Humor has traditionally been a realm where impoliteness is permitted, even in polite society, where a well-timed "just kidding" will excuse any slight. In simpler times, controversial subjects were explored safely through humor because everyone understood they were only jokes. But nowadays, people are wise to what humor really is. They know it's merely frosting on a cake, and sometimes the cake has gone bad. Every joke carries the teller's message like a Trojan Horse, even when that message is toxic.

Underhanded, hateful, or overtly cruel humor won't fly today. Even if your humor celebrates and delights in other people without bullying them, you might still offend someone once in a while. That's okay. People have a right to be offended, just as you have a right to be offensive. It doesn't mean the end of you. Humor that never offends is rare. It's also bland, has no bite, and feels committee written. Humor works best when it's a little shocking, a little inappropriate. No one is clamoring to hear the latest appropriate joke.

On the flip side, you can't predict what will offend delicate sensibilities. Sometimes the most harmless joke will lead to a sour look, an angry letter, or a hastily scheduled meeting with HR. You can't win them all. A small percentage of your audience will hate you and your humor, about 2% of them, I figure. That's part of the price of doing humor. And it's a small price to pay. Ninety-eight percent of them will love you. Those are great odds.

Canceled

Every culture gets to decide, collectively, what's appropriate and inappropriate when it comes to the humor offered up in every format from the mass media to one-on-one conversations. If you don't like the boundaries in the community you're in, find a different community.

Invariably, these decisions evolve, based on a push and pull from the humorists, audiences, and the platform gatekeepers. In the latter half of the twentieth century, comedians like Redd Foxx, Lenny Bruce, and George Carlin, as well as comedy outfits like *National Lampoon*, *The Smothers Brothers Comedy Hour*, *The Simpsons*, and *The Onion*, pushed boundaries and tested audiences' tolerance for humor on the edge of appropriateness. At many points during this evolution, police, lawyers, and Supreme Court decisions pushed back in the other direction.

In the 2010s and 2020s, the pendulum has swung far in the direction of political correctness. Although traditional swear words are now commonplace, new words and concepts are deemed much worse by younger generations. Misogynistic words, words that malign communities, and words that endanger marginalized groups are the new swear words. Ethnic slurs that used to be commonplace in humor parlance, especially on the low-brow spectrum, have become no-nos. Some survive as empowered communities reclaim the words with pride. Unawares, you might be canceled for using the same word in one context, and welcomed into a community with open arms in another.

Finding a Mooring Mast

This landscape of eggshells has scared off a lot of would-be humorists in the modern age. They've seen how a professional comedian can be pilloried by the culture at large for one of any ill-defined offenses, including even poorly aged tweets from years gone by. How can an amateur expect to survive in this environment?

Although some of us may think the pendulum has swung too far, there are several ballasts that remain unchanged throughout the storm. Many comedians whose work may have been considered inappropriate in the past still enjoy a large posthumous audience today. Many emerging humorists push boundaries and find great success today, sailing with ease through waters that are supposedly treacherous.

The concern is largely overblown. Unless you're sexually assaulting people (in which case you deserve to be canceled) or afflicting the afflicted, you don't have to worry about backlash from your humor. The world is awash in humor, from the patently filthy, cruel, and unthinkable to the most corporate-tested, lawyer-approved drivel. Your humor is a drop in the bucket.

The biggest change in recent decades is that every member of the audience now has access to the media. This is new. Prior to the internet, an ivory tower and legions of threshold guardians protected humorists from the general public. Now, anyone can tweet, post a video, or write a blog article, and anyone can go viral. Everyone can comment. Audiences have a voice. If somebody doesn't like a joke, they can tell the world. This is a good thing. People deserve a voice. Victims of sexual abuse at the hands of celebrities now have an outlet to name their accusers. This is an even better thing, and these people especially deserve a voice. Today, there are very few publicity campaigns and PR efforts that have the power to contain a scandal.

Yes, the audience is watching humorists more carefully now. Our humor is seen and heard more. We're experiencing the Big Brother prophesied by George Orwell. But it's not the government spying on us. (Well, the government is spying on us, but they don't care what we do.) We're spying on ourselves, and we very much care what we do. In this strange dystopia, those who thrive are well behaved to a point and know how to offend for effect.

Following the Rules

If you're in a highly controlled environment like a school or workplace, you're in a special kind of minefield. Here, you have legitimate cause for concern that much of the humor you may have seen from days gone by – even humor available in the media today – will not be acceptable to your overseers.

There's no shame in following the rules. Bite your tongue if you have to. Or break some rules if you want some excitement. Try to change the culture. Either way, you're free to go home, go out, and let yourself be as offensive as you want on your own time.

Best Practices

- Don't assault anyone.
- Produce your humor and share it with people without worrying that you'll get canceled.

Exercises

1. Write the most offensive jokes you can think of in a torrential session of the free writing exercise.
2. Show these jokes only to your closest confidants. You might have some gold in there.

CHAPTER

22

Make It Fun

I n this final chapter, I advise that you do something that might come as a surprise. It might seem self-sabotaging (to me, not you). That advice is to ignore everything I've told you in this book. Forget it and do whatever you want. There are no rules in humor, especially when you're learning. You have to blunder and flounder and make mistakes to get good at anything. You have to explore uncharted waters to discover what works for you. My role is to point out some of the potential pitfalls and give you some guideposts to help you along and prevent you from wasting an inordinate amount of time.

After my pile-on of rules, best practices, and dos and don'ts, the only thing you need to know to master humor is that it should be fun. If you enjoy it, you'll want to do it more, and you'll do it out of sheer joy. When you do anything out of sheer joy, you'll get good practice. And that's how you build any skill, including the skill of humor.

Whatever you do, don't burden yourself with pressure and anxiety about being funny. If you're worried about whether you're funny, you'll spend more time fretting and less time enjoying being funny, which is the point of humor.

Discover Your Own Way

You'll discover your own rights and wrongs when creating humor in your own inimitable voice, and those rights and wrongs will change with every situation, depending on the people involved, their relationships, and the context. Embrace this complexity as one of the delights of the game of humor. It's an exciting new terrain you get to explore. An unpredictable challenge now and then is the spice of life.

Make humor a riddle to figure out. What could be perceived as funny in any situation? What's funny coming from you in particular? Learn what you can from every humor attempt and apply what you learn with each successive attempt. Get a sense of when to try it and when to give it a rest. It's great to make mistakes when you're self-aware, engaged, and trying your best.

Good Luck

The tools in this book will increase your chances of creating successful humor. In the end, every attempt is still little more than a lottery ticket. When all the cylinders are firing and all the best practices are in play, sometimes things still aren't funny.

Try each chapter's exercises and approach the effort with the tips and tools you've learned, and then make your own luck. Let this book be your pocket cheat code for the humor lottery.

Have Fun

Smile at people. Be nice to grumps. Have fun with them. Be aware of their needs and encourage them to have fun, too. If people aren't laughing with joy at your humor attempts, try something else. This is the life of the humorist.

In prose, it can be difficult to know how people perceive you. Most often, you can't see them and don't know them. But you can still set the tone, as you can in any media. The tools are the same. Only the arena is different.

You start with a light tone. You drop some references to get people on your side. You show them some funny characters they recognize, and you communicate with people in your singular, extraordinary way, using the shared conventions of the language of humor, surprising them with something different while at the same time comforting them with something familiar.

You Got This

We all know how to be funny. Our species has been doing it for hundreds of thousands of years. It's baked into our DNA. It's one of our oldest and most fundamental bonding activities. We understand timing. We know just when to hide our face and then reveal it again to get a baby to laugh. We know not to play the game when the baby's bawling.

We're driven to amuse that infant. We smile to show the baby that everyone here is happy, likes them, and is having fun. When we start playing a game of peekaboo with them, we see the baby's infectious laugh bubble up. It gives us a rush of joy. It's an elemental human interaction.

We have the opportunity to bring that same peekaboo joy to the adults in our lives with a few nuanced tweaks to the game. The way we navigate the more complex social dynamics among adults is only different by degree.

We can also, from time to time, take somebody's banana.

Humor Glossary

The core of the language of humor is the funny filters. There are also terms and insider jargon humorists and comedians use with each other. Some of them are mentioned or defined in the preceding pages; others aren't. They're presented here for your reference in case you ever need to talk shop with a funny person.

Act.   A stand-up comedy performance of featured length (20 minutes to 2 hours)

Ad-lib.   To improvise a joke during a scripted performance

Audience.   The person (or persons) on the receiving end of humor

Beat.   A change of action in a story

Bit.   A prolonged joke in stand-up; a short section of a routine

Blue.   Leaning on shock topics like sex, bathroom humor, and swearing

Bomb.   To get no or few laughs from a comedy show

Button (also called *the closer*).   The closing line (often a joke) in of a piece of humor writing

Callback.   A joke that refers to another joke performed earlier, often presented in a different context

Capper.   The final joke in a bit or routine

Canned joke.   A joke in the public-domain

Canned laughter. Previously recorded laughter (or other enhancement), added after a performance

Clean. Comedy appropriate for all audiences

Closer. The closing line (often a joke) in a piece of humor writing

Die. What happens to a comedian when they perform poorly

Double entendre. A pun with one of its two meanings sexual

Dropping. Momentarily becoming a one- or two-dimensional archetype

Flopping. Bombing; not getting laughs

Funny. Humor that routinely succeeds with audiences

Gag. A joke

Gig. A short-term job

Hack. Overused and out-of-fashion material; a writer or performer who uses it

Humorist. A person delivering humor

Improv/improvisation. Making up performance material on the spot in front of an audience

In-joke (also *room joke* or *band joke*). A joke referring to information only a select subgroup is privy to

Joke. Any short funny phrase

Joke beat. A joke along a similar track of humor that escalates the bit or piece

Jokey. Material that is obvious and hacky

Kill. To give a great comedy performance

Mapping. Applying the details of one thing onto another in an analogy

One-liner. A joke made up of only one or two sentences, often strung together with other one-liners

Piece. A short comedy article or essay

Punch (punchline). The second part of a joke that gets a laugh, containing a payoff of the first part

Punching down. Joking at the expense of the disadvantaged, downtrodden, or oppressed

Punching up. Joking at the expense of the established, the powerful, and the oppressive

Riffing. Verbally escalating a humor premise

Runner. A short joke or scene repeated more than once in a script

Satire. A piece of humorous material that ridicules society or human behavior

Schtick. A comic scene or piece of business; often implying physical comedy

Set. A stand-up comedy performance of shorter length (5 to 20 minutes)

Setup. The first part of a joke that often isn't meant to be funny

Tag. An additional punch immediately following a punch that doesn't require a new setup

Take. A comedic facial reaction; the direction of a piece

Yes-anding. The primary tool of improv in which one performer accepts the reality created by another performer and adds to it

Acknowledgments

I wish to acknowledge everyone who played peekaboo with me as a baby. My mom, grandma, and everyone who was entertained against all reason by my early works of comedy. My elementary school comedy cohort, Marcellus Hall. My junior-high comedy buddies, Vince Taylor and Mark Leonard. Also Richard McClung and Troy Whipple, who laughed at us and built our confidence. My high school comedy colleagues, Peter Hilleren and Keith Webster. Humor expert Jay Rath, cartoonist and mover-and-shaker-extraordinaire James Sturm. My radio comedy cohorts, Kathryn Lake, Tracey Reece, and P.S. Mueller. All the writing staff, owners, founders, and other employees of *The Onion*, with special appreciation for Tim Keck, Chris Johnson, Richard Dahm, Pete Haise, Heather Eakey, Christine Wenc, Dan Vebber, Sean Mulheron, Sean Lafleur, Todd Hanson, Mike Loew, Nick Gallo, Michael Hirsch, Andy Selsberg, Ben Karlin, Rob Siegel, Kelly Ambrose, Carol Kolb, Maria Schneider, John Krewson, Peter Koechley, Chris Karwowski, Joe Garden, Seth Reiss, Dan Guterman, Megan Ganz, Mike DiCenzo, Joe Randazzo,

Amie Barrodale, and Chad Nackers. To say nothing of Will Graham, Dan Mirk, Lang Fischer, Beth Newell, Chris Kelly, Sam West, and so many others on the *Onion News Network* staff. The entire staff of The Second City Training Center in Chicago. All the interns, helpers, employees, and freelancers who've boosted my career. Manager David Miner; agents Jeff Herman, Dan Greenberg, Mike Lubin, Mark Gottlieb, Scott Kaufman, and Steve Roy. The entire staff at Wiley, particularly editors Brian Neil and Tom Dinse. My team, Celeste Chan, Rachel Keller, Kevin Coutu, Tammara Buckey, and Liam O'Malley. My partner, Dandelion Blume. I would be remiss not to thank Keith Sherman, Andy Richter, Conan O'Brien, Bob Odenkirk, and Amy Poehler for their support and encouragement, as well as Dr. Seuss, Jim Henson, Frank Oz, Al Feldstein, Carol Burnett, Sherwood Schwartz, Douglas Adams, Kurt Vonnegut, Monty Python, Merrill Markoe, David Letterman, Steve Martin, Andy Kaufman, Jay Leno, William Steig, and Doug Kenney for their unwitting influence.

I appreciate anyone who's ever been in my audience, on my email list, read my books or comic strips, seen me perform, taken my comedy classes, joined my Facebook groups, or subscribed to my daily newsletter, *No Dikkering Around* on Substack.

Nothing is done in solitude. You're all essential to this book.

About the Author

Scott Dikkers is *The Onion*'s longest-serving editor-in-chief and former co-owner. A number one *New York Times* bestselling author, comedy writer, and performer, Scott is widely regarded as one of the most influential pioneers in comedy history. His visionary leadership at *The Onion*, his groundbreaking comic strip *Jim's Journal*, plus his multiple top-10 comedy podcasts, radio productions, and film and TV work, have garnered him tens of millions of fans around the world. *Rolling Stone* named him one of its top 10 favorite writers. *Entertainment Weekly* designated him "the funniest person in America" and placed him on the "It List" of the hottest celebrities in show business. He graced the cover of *Time* magazine as one of the top 50 movers and shakers online. He's the winner of the Thurber Prize for American Humor, a Peabody, and more Webby awards than any other individual or organization. Scott literally wrote the book on professional comedy writing, the bestselling *How to Write Funny*, which spawned a training center at the famed Second City in Chicago and a series of online courses at howtowritefunny.com, where he continues to mentor humor writers and performers, several of whom have gone on to win Emmys, Grammys, and Oscars.

Index